Software Development Metrics

Software Development Metrics

DAVID NICOLETTE

MANNING
SHELTER ISLAND

Manning Publications Co.
20 Baldwin Road
PO Box 761
Shelter Island, NY 11964

Development editor:	Cynthia Kane
Technical development editor:	Mark Elston
Copyeditor:	Tiffany Taylor
Proofreader:	Barbara Mirecki
Typesetter:	Dottie Marsico
Cover designer:	Marija Tudor

ISBN 9781617291357
Printed in the United States of America
1 2 3 4 5 6 7 8 9 10 – EBM – 20 19 18 17 16 15

To Lourdes and Alejandro

It took several years to prepare this small book, and there were many occasions when I was strongly tempted to abandon the project. My wife Lourdes and my son Alejandro were consistently supportive. The fact this book was completed is due largely to their loving and steadfast encouragement.

contents

foreword

Years back, I noticed that Dave Nicolette's blog had the same subtitle as mine, "Effective Software Development." This contrasted subtly with what seemed to be the dominant interest at the time, *efficient* software development. I quickly found out that even when our opinions differed, our goals and values tended to be in close alignment, and the conversations were always enlightening.

I've worked with a number of organizations, large and small, in a decade of being an independent software development consultant. This work has given me opportunity to observe these organizations in action. The ones that are most stuck are the ones that focus on efficiency.

Efficiency tends to squeeze the slack out and discourages taking time to wonder and explore. This single-mindedness eliminates the opportunity to learn. Learning is reduced to optimizing measures within the local neighborhood of the status quo, often to the detriment of valuable things less easily measured. Companies set up systems to gather this data efficiently, sometimes at the expense of veracity. If the metrics mania takes hold, they may have programmers take time from programming to collect more data, blindly sacrificing efficiency in real work on the altar of efficiency in measuring the work.

I've seen other companies initiate a metrics program because … well, because it's the thing to do. It will improve their process, or enable them to manage scientifically, or attain some other vague goal. They generally try to measure as much as is convenient to capture. They often start with every metric that their toolset makes available, but they don't have a clear idea of what to do with the numbers they collect. In fact, I've seen cases where nobody ever looked at the numbers. They just found collecting numbers reassuring, like a child playing with a teddy bear.

As they mature just a little, organizational metrics programs start to develop goals for their measurements. I've seen obsession with efficiency accompanied with using metrics to ensure they are maximizing the productivity indicators that they can easily measure. I've seen people collect measures to confirm what they already believe. I've seen them overlook data that might invalidate beliefs or assumptions. I've seen them ignore data they have, because it's not in a form that's convenient to quantify. I've seen them use metrics to set targets for managers and workers, falling victim to Goodhart's Law—a metric used as a target ceases to function as a measurement.

There are so many ways that we can use metrics to lead ourselves astray. It's easy to depend on them to make our decisions for us, rather than use them to illuminate reality so we can make better decisions. The common problems with metrics programs make it tempting to do away with them.

Unfortunately, we can fool ourselves just as easily with anecdotes. Measuring things can be a great way to double-check our beliefs. Measurements can also uncover phenomena that we hadn't otherwise noticed.

So I had great interest when Dave told me he was working on a book about metrics. I knew it wouldn't be a run-of-the-mill, shortsighted book. And, indeed, it is not. Dave describes here how to use metrics to do our bidding, rather than to be our masters.

This is an opinionated book. Dave does not catalog all of the metrics he knows. He dwells on the ones he finds effective. With each of these, he not only tells us when it's appropriate and how to use it well, but cautions us about how it can lead us astray if we use it clumsily. In addition, he cautions against a couple metrics that are not helpful for steering software development projects.

In this book, Dave concentrates on two goals of using metrics: steering a software development project to success, and improving the process of software development. He provides practical advice on how to meet these goals, advice grounded in years of experience. There are examples of using multiple metrics to derive insights into the development process, to stabilize the predictability of planning, and to report upwards in the management chain. This book will be a helpful guide to most project managers and team leads, and a real boon to those making a transition from a traditional serial development model to an agile one.

GEORGE DINWIDDIE
SOFTWARE DEVELOPMENT CONSULTANT AND COACH

preface

Every published software development process includes recommended metrics to use with that process. So why would anyone bother to write a book like this one? Is there any use for this book?

Well, have you ever discovered a software-delivery issue very late in the game, when it was too late to deal with the issue effectively? Have you ever believed you were tracking the right information to stay ahead of delivery issues, but surprises still came up? You're not alone. From the earliest days of digital computers to the present day, people have been looking for reliable ways to detect potential delivery issues early enough to act on them. People still have difficulty understanding what to measure and what to do with the numbers they collect.

In my consulting work, at conferences and user group meetings, in online discussions, and in reading published material on the subject of software metrics, I often encounter people who are frustrated with the challenges of measuring software development and delivery work. They measure more and more things and generate more and more charts and graphs, and yet surprises still occur. Over the past 10 years or so, I've noticed a common denominator in these cases: people aren't measuring what is really happening in their organizations; they're measuring what they think is happening, or what they believe should be happening based on the labels and buzz-words people use to describe their process.

During my experiences in helping teams and organizations improve their software-delivery performance, it has become clear to me that most people have no idea what to measure. They try to use the metrics that are recommended for the published processes they've adopted, and they find that those metrics don't help them steer the work or quantify process improvements. Teams are repeatedly blindsided by unexpected delivery risks late in the delivery cycle. Their metrics fail to provide early warning of delivery risks.

When I began to give talks at conferences and user-group meetings on the subject of software development metrics, I was surprised to find standing-room-only crowds who were loathe to leave the room at the end of the time slot. Presentations and demonstrations of software development metrics repeatedly drew audiences like that. There seemed to be a general lack of understanding of what to measure, how to measure it, and what to do with the results. I began to collect information about metrics that I had used effectively with software development teams, and metrics that colleagues in the field had used.

A common problem I encounter in the field is that people aren't sure how to determine which metrics will be helpful in their context. Not every metric applies to every software delivery process. Based on observation and experience, I came up with a simple model that identifies key characteristics of different software delivery processes, regardless of the buzzwords people use to describe their process or the published framework people believe they are following. Based on that model, people can identify the metrics that may help them and the metrics that probably won't help them.

There were, and still are, many references about metrics that approach the topic from a theoretical or statistical perspective. Although these are interesting and possibly useful on an academic level, people involved with software delivery generally find them hard to apply to everyday work. It occurred to me that it might be useful to compile some of the practical information about metrics in a central place and to organize the information around common real-world situations.

I was familiar with Manning as a technical publisher, and I had found practical value in several of the company's books, so I thought it might be a practical-minded publisher for information about software metrics. I discussed the idea of the book with folks at Manning, and they were interested in pursuing it. The project took much longer than I expected, but at long last here is the result. The goal was to prepare a sort of "survival guide" for people close to the work who need to detect potential delivery risks early in the delivery process, or who want to quantify the effects of their process-improvement efforts.

Toward that end, this book presents a compilation of practical metrics to help steer software development work, to track delivery performance, and to monitor the effects of process improvement efforts. It isn't based on abstract theory, statistical methods, or earlier literature about software metrics. It focuses on ground-level work and doesn't deal with enterprise-level measurement.

The book also presents a number of anti-patterns, or common mis-applications of metrics. All too often, when we measure the "wrong" things, we create unintended incentives for people to behave in counterproductive ways. It's useful to be aware of the potential behavioral effects of metrics.

There's another use for metrics, besides tracking progress toward a goal. We're often interested in improvement: changes in organizational structure, role definitions, arrangement of team workspaces, process, methods, collaboration, technical practices, tools, collocation versus remote work, or something else. Many people change things without measuring the impact of the changes. Others measure the rate of adoption of new practices, but not the impact of the new practices on results. Some metrics can help us understand whether the changes we try are actually improving our delivery effectiveness, the quality of our software, or the quality of our working lives.

My hope is that this book presents this information in a way that you will find easy to put to use in your own development processes.

acknowledgments

This book summarizes lessons learned in the field. It's hard to say where each lesson came from; I haven't been keeping track of that over the years. In some cases, I happen to know who created (or first published) a given metric. Those individuals are named in the text. Some are professional colleagues who do the same sort of work as I do; others were client personnel who came up with practical metrics in their own context. If I tried to recall all the names, I would surely forget a few and they might be offended. So it's better not to name names. In most cases, I don't know who created the metrics or exactly where I learned them.

It's easier to acknowledge those who directly encouraged me to complete the book. First on that list is my wife Lourdes, who encouraged me to keep at it nearly every day for the past few years. Some of my friends and colleagues were aware that I was working on the book, and they also nagged me on a fairly regular basis to complete it.

I must say that Manning had a great deal to do with the fact this book ever saw the light of day. The folks there talked me out of abandoning the project on more than one occasion. I burned through two of their editors before finding one who could get the work out of me: Cynthia Kane. Special thanks to her and everyone else on the Manning team who worked with me during the writing and publication process. Thank you also to George Dinwiddie for contributing the foreword to my book.

Finally, thanks to the many MEAP (Manning Early Access Program) readers who posted comments and corrections in the book's forum, and to the following reviewers who provided invaluable feedback on the manuscript during its development: Andrew Gibson, Ajay George, Avijit Das, Christopher Davis, Efran Cobisi, Frances Buontempo, Furkan Kamaci, Gary Pollice, Gavin Baumanis, John Booth, Marcin Kawalerowicz, Michael Benner, Philippe Charrière, Ricardo da Paz, and Shaun Lippy.

about this book

Metrics are a necessary evil. Measurement is easily the least interesting aspect of software development, and yet without it we have little chance of delivering anything useful. But nearly everyone I meet in the software field is at a loss to know what to measure or how to use the measurements. The standard metrics we all learn in school often fail to help us in the real world. Whenever I give a talk about metrics, the room is filled beyond capacity and people stay beyond the allotted time. I'm always surprised, because this isn't an inherently interesting subject. People need practical metrics that are a fit for their situations. I can't claim this book will be a fun read, but I do think it fills a gap that sorely needs to be filled.

This book approaches the topic differently than others. It's neither an academic study of metrics nor a survey of existing literature nor a sales pitch for metrics intended to accompany a published software-delivery framework. Rather, it's process-agnostic and offers advice to help you recognize how the work flows in your organization, regardless of labels and buzzwords, so you can choose or create metrics that can help you steer development work toward a goal or quantify the effects of improvement efforts. The book doesn't ask you to change your organization; it's meant to help you survive in the organization as it currently exists. It doesn't suggest what you should measure, but rather what you can measure in light of present organizational realities.

Roadmap

Chapter 1 reviews a few fundamentals about measurement and metrics and introduces a practical model for understanding how work flows in an organization. This model can then be the basis for selecting metrics appropriate to your situation. There's a brief description of the two purposes of metrics—to steer work in progress and to guide improvement efforts—and the three functions of metrics—informational, diagnostic, and motivational—and a review of some basic concepts like leading and trailing indicators. Then a few concepts are introduced that may be less familiar, such as the notion of forward-facing and backward-facing metrics, and the idea of pragmatic measurement.

The chapter covers the differences between traditional and adaptive development, which needs clarification because many people conflate these concepts with specific process frameworks or methodologies. I also describe four reference models for software-delivery processes. By correlating your reality with these reference models, you can select appropriate metrics for your context. Finally, the differences between running discrete projects and doing continuous delivery are described. This factor also has an influence on your choice of metrics.

Chapter 2 describes metrics that are useful for steering work in progress. They're presented in no particular order, except that metrics relevant to traditional development are presented first, and metrics relevant to adaptive development appear later. The order of presentation implies nothing about which approach you "should" use. They're loosely grouped that way so you won't have to go on a scavenger hunt to find the metrics that apply to the way in which software is delivered in your organization.

In chapter 2, I use a template at the beginning of each section to help you recognize whether that particular metric is of interest to you. That way, you can skip the sections that aren't relevant in your context without wasting a lot of time reading. The template contains the following:

- *Question(s) answered*—What questions can this metric help you answer?
- *Description*—A brief description of the metric.
- *Value*—What kinds of value can you obtain from using the metric?
- *Dependencies*—Traditional versus adaptive approach, process model, and delivery mode for which the metric is meaningful.
- *Success factors*—Any special considerations that must be met for the metric to serve its purpose properly.

For most metrics, chapter 2 describes common abuses, or anti-patterns. The anti-patterns can give you a sense of how the misapplication of a metric can lead to negative outcomes. This may help you use the metrics appropriately. I'm not aware of any other published material about metrics that even acknowledges misapplication is possible, let alone describes how it can happen. I suspect this is because most books about metrics are trying to sell you the metrics the author happens to like or those that are supposed to be used with the process framework the book proposes you use. This book is only meant to help you select and apply metrics that fit your context. I explicitly avoid recommending any process framework or methodology. I do have opinions about that, but that isn't the purpose of this book.

Chapter 3 is about metrics that can be useful in guiding and quantifying process-improvement efforts. This can be a bit more complicated than tracking progress toward a delivery goal. To achieve improvement, you must change your development practices and delivery methods. You need to be aware of process dependencies that can break metrics when you change your process. The chapter also explains how some metrics can be used to track progress and to quantify improvement, and how to use them for each purpose. In addition, two categories of metrics apply to measuring improvement but have no role in tracking delivery. Technical metrics help you understand the quality of your code base. Human metrics help you understand how team members feel about their work; it turns out this is important for effective delivery.

Chapter 4 assembles some of the building blocks presented in chapters 2 and 3 to show how multiple metrics of different types can shed more light on a situation than any single metric alone. It would be impractical to include every conceivable combination of metrics that you might apply. I've tried to make the chapter useful by focusing on patterns that I've seen many times in industry. These may be of direct use to you because they're so common. I hope they also provide examples you can use to combine other metrics in practical ways.

Chapter 5 focuses on a single aspect of managing software-development work: predictable short-term planning. Metrics play a large role in planning. Stakeholders appreciate predictability more than they appreciate speed of delivery. They will accept reduced scope more readily than they will accept repeated disappointment. Many, if not most, people involved in software development have a great deal of difficulty with predictability. Many teams resort to guesswork; gut-feel predictions; bottom-up, time-based estimation; coerced "commitments"; or just plain hope to determine how much work they can deliver in the next stage of delivery. None of those methods is effective. This chapter describes various ways to achieve predictable short-term planning based on measurement and discusses pitfalls of doing it wrong.

Chapter 6 deals with your interaction with the organization beyond your own team or teams. What do senior management and business stakeholders need to know, and what do they not need to know? How can you provide the information they require with a minimum of effort on your part and without disrupting your teams' ability to stay focused on the technical work? Some organizations define standard metrics they require from all projects. Some of those metrics may be completely meaningless. If I assume you aren't in a position to change those standards, you can at least recognize which metrics are worthy of your time and which aren't.

Downloadable spreadsheet

A spreadsheet accompanies this book and is available for download from the publisher's website at www.manning.com/software-development-metrics. The spreadsheet contains the base data and formulae for most of the metrics described in the book.

Who should read this book?

This book is meant for people who are on the front lines of software delivery and who want to be prepared to answer questions about progress and/or about improvements in delivery effectiveness. Job titles vary, and there's no single title that unambiguously identifies a person who might benefit from the book. In a traditional environment, the title Project Manager or Line Manager often describes a person in this position; but sometimes these titles denote higher positions (that is, disconnected from the day-to-day work). In organizations that use a more contemporary approach to software delivery, titles like Team Lead, Project Lead, Technical Lead, Scrum Master, Iteration Manager, Delivery Manager, and Delivery Lead may be used. In organizations that apply the concept of self-organizing teams, there may be no specific job title with responsibility for tracking progress, and it's a shared responsibility or a rotating responsibility of team members.

Whatever their titles, the book is for people who have direct responsibility for delivery for one or more teams and who are in direct touch with the day-to-day work. It offers help in using metrics to answer questions like, "Are we delivering what stakeholders need?" "Are we going to run out of money?" "Are we going to run out of time?" "How much of the planned scope can we deliver by date X?" and "Has our latest process change resulted in improved delivery performance?"

It may be easier to describe people who *aren't* the target audience. The book isn't aimed at mid-level or upper-level IT managers or business stakeholders of the IT department. It doesn't deal with program-level or enterprise-level measurement and tracking.

Author Online

The purchase of *Software Development Metrics* includes free access to a private web forum run by Manning Publications, where you can make comments about the book, ask technical questions, and receive help from the author and from other users. To access the forum and subscribe to it, point your web browser to www.manning.com/software-development-metrics. This page provides information on how to get on the forum once you are registered, what kind of help is available, and the rules of conduct on the forum.

Manning's commitment to our readers is to provide a venue where a meaningful dialogue between individual readers and between readers and the author can take place. It isn't a commitment to any specific amount of participation on the part of the author, whose contribution to the forum remains voluntary (and unpaid). We suggest you try asking the author some challenging questions lest his interest stray!

The Author Online forum and the archives of previous discussions will be accessible from the publisher's web site as long as the book is in print.

About the author

Dave Nicolette has worked in the software development field since 1977. He has undertaken many roles associated with software development and delivery, and has used most of the well-known processes and methodologies, from traditional SDLC to contemporary lightweight methods. Since 1984, Dave has worked mainly as a contractor or consultant. As a result, he has experienced a wide variety of software-development environments, methods, and tools. This experience gives him practical, ground-level insights into the conditions that enable a given measurement to provide useful information.

About the cover illustration

The figure on the cover of *Software Development Metrics* is captioned "Man from the Island of Mljet, Croatia." The illustration is taken from a reproduction of an album of traditional Croatian costumes from the mid-nineteenth century by Nikola Arsenovic, published by the Ethnographic Museum in Split, Croatia, in 2003. The illustrations were obtained from a helpful librarian at the museum, which is situated in the Roman core of the medieval center of the town: the ruins of Emperor Diocletian's retirement palace from around AD 304. The book includes finely colored illustrations of figures from different regions of Croatia, accompanied by descriptions of the costumes and of everyday life.

Mljet is the most southerly and easterly in a string of islands in the Adriatic Sea that belong to Croatia. The island is sparsely populated and large swaths of it are covered by forests that are part of a national park. The figure on the cover is dressed in the everyday costume typical for this region—dark blue wool pants, a black vest over a white linen shirt, and a large black hat that completes the outfit. He is smoking a pipe and holding a long-handled axe used for cutting brush and firewood.

Dress codes and lifestyles have changed over the last 200 years, and the diversity by region, so rich at the time, has faded away. It is now hard to tell apart the inhabitants of different continents, let alone of different hamlets or towns separated by only a few miles. Perhaps we have traded cultural diversity for a more varied personal life—certainly for a more varied and fast-paced technological life.

Manning celebrates the inventiveness and initiative of the computer business with book covers based on the rich diversity of regional life of two centuries ago, brought back to life by illustrations from old books and collections like this one.

Making metrics useful

This chapter covers

- The difference between measurements and metrics
- What we mean by *pragmatic* metrics
- Trailing and leading indicators
- The purpose and functions of metrics
- Factors to consider when choosing metrics

This book is designed for a person at the bottom of the management hierarchy in a software development organization. A person in such a position usually has direct responsibility for delivery as well as management duties at the team level. In a traditional organization, this role is usually called Project Manager. In contemporary organizations, people with similar responsibilities may have a title like Team Lead, Development Lead, Delivery Lead, Scrum Master, or Iteration Manager. In a peer-based, self-organizing team, these responsibilities may be shared across all team members.

The purpose of the book is to provide practical guidance to people who need to steer work in progress and who want to measure the effectiveness of process-improvement efforts. It offers a way to do so that doesn't depend on popular buzz-words and doesn't require the work to be done in any particular way. It suggests what can be measured based on organizational realities, and not necessarily what should be measured in an ideal world.

Anything you do in the course of your work ought to have a clear purpose. Otherwise, you're just performing random activities in order to stay busy. Metrics for software development have a couple of purposes. First, you can use them to judge how well you're tracking toward the goals of a project. Second, you can use metrics to help you understand whether you're improving your delivery performance.

With that in mind, metrics can help with the following:

- Steering work in progress
- Guiding process improvements

Software development and delivery is usually carried out either as a discrete project that has a beginning and an end, or as an ongoing activity for evolutionary development or production support. In either case, there are expectations about how the work will progress. You need to know, as early as possible, when actual performance is diverging from expected performance so that you can take appropriate corrective action. I think of this action as steering the work: directing the work toward a goal.

It has become the norm for software professionals to assess their own practices and methods almost continuously, and to try to improve the way they do their work. Metrics can be useful to help you understand when a change leads to improvement and when it doesn't. Metrics can also help you make a case to change formal methods based on quantitative results from using a proposed new approach.

This chapter sets the stage for our examination of metrics for software development. To choose metrics appropriate to your work context, you need to know what decisions you're trying to support through metrics. You also need to understand how each metric is affected by a few key factors, such as whether you're taking a traditional or adaptive approach to development, what sort of process model you're using, and whether you're running discrete projects or carrying out continuous development and support.

1.1 *Measurements and metrics*

A *measurement* is a quantitative observation of one of the following:

- Something relevant to the decisions you have to make
- Information you have to report regarding the progress of development
- The effects of process improvements

A *metric* is a recurring measurement that has informational, diagnostic, motivational, or predictive power of some kind. It helps you understand whether you're at risk of missing expected results, or whether changes in process or practices are resulting in improved performance.

1.1.1 *What makes a metric "pragmatic"?*

Sometimes, managers get a bit carried away with metrics. They track all the metrics they can think of, or all the metrics their favorite project-management tool happens to support. They may or may not be able to tell you just why they're tracking any given metric. That sort of thing isn't practical; it's busywork. It's better to be pragmatic about measurement—that is, to have a clear purpose in mind for each metric you use.

There is effort and cost involved in collecting data and tracking metrics. To justify this cost, any metrics you use must have a practical purpose. A metric is *pragmatic* if it provides information that helps a stakeholder make a decision.

People usually think of the customer of a software product as the primary or only stakeholder of the software development project. For the purposes of this book, *you* are the main stakeholder, because you're the party with primary responsibility for tracking progress. Your management, other departments in your company, and members of the development team are also stakeholders.

Ideally, any metrics you track will help at least one of these stakeholders make decisions of one kind or another. Customers may make decisions about scope and schedule depending on how the work is progressing. Management may make decisions about portfolio management and budget allocations. Team members may make decisions about how to improve their delivery effectiveness. You may make decisions about how to steer work in progress.

All too often, project managers track metrics just because they can, or just because "it's always been done that way." I've seen managers get carried away with graphics or query options offered by their project-management software. I've seen others track metrics that don't apply to the work they're managing, because they used the same metrics on previous projects where those metrics *did* apply. And I've seen managers use metrics that formally belong to the methodology they *think* they're using, when in fact the work isn't done according to that methodology. I want to encourage you to consider the practical purpose of any metrics you choose to use, and to avoid creating extra work for yourself by collecting data that won't or can't be used to support decisions.

TRAILING AND LEADING INDICATORS

We're interested in measuring things that have already happened as well as predicting things that are likely to happen in the future. Measurements of things that have already happened can often help us predict how things are likely to progress going forward.

Any metric that provides information about things that have already happened is considered a *trailing indicator* or *lagging indicator*. Any metric that helps us predict how things will happen in the future is considered a *leading indicator*. A leading indicator often comprises a series of trailing indicators along with a calculated trend that suggests how things are likely to play out, provided circumstances remain stable.

FUNCTIONS OF METRICS

Metrics have three functions, or effects:

- Informational
- Diagnostic
- Motivational

When a metric provides plain information, it serves an informational function. When a metric calls attention to a problem, it serves a diagnostic function. When a metric influences people's behavior, it serves a motivational function. Metrics may perform in more than one of these ways at the same time and can have effects that you didn't intend or plan—especially motivational effects.

1.1.2 *Forward-facing and backward-facing metrics*

There are a couple of different general approaches to software development and delivery. The *traditional approach* involves a thorough analysis of stakeholder needs, a comprehensive solution design, a careful assessment of risks, and a fixed budget allocation in advance. The *adaptive approach* involves defining a vision for the desired future state, performing sufficient analysis to get started, and exploring the solution space in collaboration with stakeholders through incremental delivery and frequent feedback.

Many metrics boil down to a comparison between expected and actual performance. With the traditional approach, the definition of expectations is in the comprehensive project plan that's created before development begins. As development progresses, the definition of success (the project plan) lies in the past. Even when a plan is re-baselined, the new plan lies in the past, from the perspective of the development team. I think of metrics that support traditional development as *backward-facing* metrics, because you have to face the past in order to see your target (see figure 1.1).

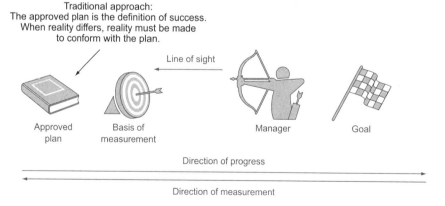

Figure 1.1 **Traditional development: you must face the past to see your target.**

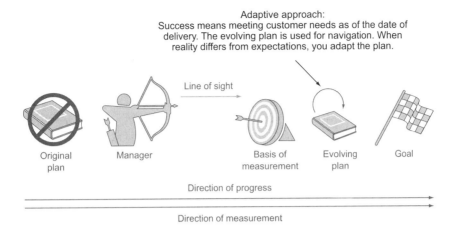

Figure 1.2 **Adaptive development: you must face the future to see your target.**

With the adaptive approach, the definition of expectations is the point-in-time understanding of the future-state vision as of today. This understanding evolves day by day as development progresses. I think of metrics that support adaptive development as *forward-facing* metrics, because you have to face the future in order to see your target (see figure 1.2).

For the purpose of choosing meaningful metrics, the key distinction is the way the *triple constraint* or *iron triangle* of scope, schedule, and budget is managed. With the traditional approach, the scope, schedule, and budget are all fully defined in advance. Metrics are used to track the development team's performance compared with the plan.

With the adaptive approach, one or two of these factors are left flexible on purpose. Metrics are used to assess whether the scope, schedule, or budget has to be adjusted to keep the work on track toward the future-state vision. Some metrics are meaningful only with one approach or the other.

1.2 *Factors affecting the choice of metrics*

In addition to the general approach—traditional or adaptive development—you also have to consider the *process model* and *delivery mode* you're using to develop and deliver the solution.

1.2.1 *Process model*

The sort of development process you're using will influence your choice of metrics. Some metrics depend on the work being done in a certain way. A common problem is that people believe they're using a given process, when in fact they're working according to a conflicting set of assumptions. If you apply metrics that depend on the process being done correctly, you won't obtain information that can help you steer the

work or measure the results of process-improvement efforts. You have to measure
what's *really* happening, regardless of the buzzwords people use to label it.

Countless published and home-grown processes are in use to build and deliver
software. In my experience, they all boil down to just four basic reference models:

- *Linear*—Based on the assumption that software development must proceed in
  order through a distinct series of steps. The steps include activities such as business analysis, requirements specification, solution design, coding, testing,
  deployment, and support. The linear process model is sometimes called a *waterfall* process, because work can't flow backward any more than water can flow
  uphill.

- *Iterative*—Based on the assumption that a single pass through the requirements
  is unlikely to result in a good solution. With an iterative process, the requirements are revisited time and again, and the solution is built up through a series
  of iterations. This may involve progressive refinement of the solution, gradual
  addition of specific features, or a combination.

- *Time-boxed*—The same as the iterative model, with the addition of two defining
  characteristics: (1) each iteration is the same length, and (2) a potentially ship-
  pable increment (or *vertical slice*) of the solution is delivered by the end of each
  time-boxed iteration.

- *Continuous flow*—Based on the assumption that the most effective way to keep
  work moving forward is to focus on maintaining a continuous flow, usually by
  controlling the level of work in process (WIP) and using techniques adapted
  from the Lean school of thought.

All real-world processes are based primarily on one of these four reference models
and include elements from one or more of the remaining three. You can usually use
metrics that apply to the reference model that is closest to the actual process you're
using. As this is written, the iterative model is the most widely used and has the largest
range of variations in practice.

If your organization is typical, then a couple of things are probably true:

- More than one process model is in use.
- Each process model in your organization is a hybrid model.

Software organizations of any appreciable size almost always apply different processes
to different types of work, depending on the nature of the work. For example, you
might use a linear process for highly predictable, routine projects; an iterative or
time-boxed process for work that has to do with creating or maintaining competitive
advantage; and a continuous-flow process for production support and infrastructure
support.

In addition, only a vanishingly small number of organizations use any given process exactly as it's defined in books. Processes are almost always customized to the
needs of the particular organization. Sometimes the modifications are well-reasoned

adjustments that take into account the local realities of the organization. Other times they're the result of misunderstanding how a process is meant to work, particularly when it's a relatively new process that's just becoming popular.

This book takes no sides on those issues. As a practical matter, the important thing for you is to be able to recognize how your work really flows and which metrics might help you steer.

1.2.2 Delivery mode

Software is built, delivered, and supported in one of two ways: as discrete projects or as ongoing development and support. A project has a start date and an end date. Between those dates, a team strives to achieve one or more goals—delivering a set of application features or standing up an IT asset. Some organizations form a new team for each project, whereas others assign projects to stable teams. Projects are often treated as capital investments and budgeted accordingly.

In an ongoing development and support mode, application or infrastructure features are delivered incrementally on an ongoing basis. Applications or technical assets are usually supported by the same team that enhances them. Ongoing work is often treated as an operating expense and budgeted accordingly.

In a corporate IT department, production support and operations are usually managed as ongoing support, whereas application development and new infrastructure features are usually managed as discrete projects. But ongoing delivery is also feasible for application development. Many internet-based email services, online catalog sales systems, social media sites, and other types of applications are developed and supported in an ongoing mode that has no planned ending date, sometimes called *continuous beta*. Some companies are finding this mode works well for all kinds of IT work and are moving away from discrete projects altogether.

Some metrics are sensitive to this factor and are meaningful with only one of these two options. The largest challenge when choosing metrics for steering work is the case when the same team has ongoing support responsibilities combined with project work—not unusual for infrastructure teams.

1.3 How the metrics are presented

Chapters 2 and 3 deal with individual metrics in isolation. We'll cover the purpose, mechanics, enabling factors, and common anti-patterns (inappropriate uses) of each metric. This is the format I'll use to describe each metric:

Name of the metric

Question(s) answered
- What does this metric tell us? It tells us *this* and *that*.

Description
- A brief description of the metric Value
- The value we can obtain by using the metric

Dependencies
- Approach: traditional or adaptive
- Process model: linear, iterative, time-boxed, continuous flow, or any
- Delivery mode: discrete project or continuous development

Success factors
- Special considerations above and beyond the basic dependencies

1.4 Summary

In this chapter, you learned the following:

- A *measurement* is a point-in-time observation of a single data point, whereas a *metric* comprises recurring measurements organized in a way that's designed to provide information useful for making decisions about your work.

- You use metrics for two purposes: to help steer work in progress and to help monitor the effectiveness of process-improvement efforts.

- Metrics have three *functions* or *effects*: informational, diagnostic, and motivational. Any metric can perform more than one of these functions simultaneously. Metrics often have a motivational effect even when you don't intend it.

- Your choice of metrics depends on three general factors: the *approach* (traditional or adaptive), the *process model* (linear, iterative, time-boxed, or continuous flow), and the *delivery mode* (discrete project or continuous evolution/support).

- The definition of success in traditional software development is to conform closely to a project plan developed in the past, sticking to the originally defined scope, schedule, and budget. Because the target lies in the past, to track progress you must use *backward-facing* metrics.

- The definition of success in adaptive software development is to deliver the business value that stakeholders require at the time they need it, at the appropriate level of quality, and at the right price point. Because the target lies in the future, to track progress you must use *forward-facing* metrics.

Metrics for steering

This chapter covers

- The purpose and mechanics of several metrics
- Dependencies of each metric
- Common anti-patterns or inappropriate uses metrics

In this chapter, I'll describe the purpose and mechanics of a number of metrics that are useful for helping you steer your work. I'll explain what sorts of questions each metric answers, as well as the implications of development approach, process model, and delivery mode on the meaning and usefulness of the metric. Finally, I'll mention a few abuses, or *anti-patterns*, that often occur when people misapply the metric.

This chapter is longer than the rest, because there is a good deal of material to cover on the subject of metrics for steering. The chapter is designed to guide you to metrics that may be helpful in your context. It isn't meant to be read straight through, like a novel.

First, assess your situation in light of the three factors introduced previously:

- *Development approach*
  - Traditional
  - Adaptive

- *Process model*
  - Linear
  - Iterative
  - Time-boxed
  - Continuous flow
- *Delivery mode*
  - Discrete projects
  - Ongoing or continuous

Then decide which metrics are worthy of your attention by scanning the "Dependencies" in the summary that introduces each section of the chapter. Read about the metrics that align with the characteristics of your work flow, and skip the others. Table 2.1 provides an overview of how the metrics align with the three key characteristics of work flow. It may help you identify which sections of the chapter you want to read.

Table 2.1   Metrics cross-reference

Metric	Approach	Process model	Delivery mode
Percentage of scope complete	• Traditional • Adaptive (with fixed scope)	• Linear • Iterative • Time-boxed • Continuous flow	• Project
Earned value	• Traditional	• Linear • Iterative • Time-boxed • Continuous flow	• Project
Budget burn	• Traditional • Adaptive	• Linear • Iterative • Time-boxed • Continuous flow	• Project
Buffer burn rate	• Traditional • Adaptive	• Linear • Iterative • Time-boxed • Continuous flow	• Project
Running tested features	• Adaptive	• Iterative • Time-boxed • Continuous flow	• Project
Earned business value	• Adaptive	• Iterative • Time-boxed • Continuous flow	• Project

Table 2.1   **Metrics cross-reference** *(continued)*

Metric	Approach	Process model	Delivery mode
Velocity	▪ Traditional ▪ Adaptive	▪ Time-boxed	▪ Project
Cycle time	▪ Traditional ▪ Adaptive	▪ Linear ▪ Iterative ▪ Time-boxed ▪ Continuous flow	▪ Project ▪ Ongoing
Burn chart	▪ Traditional ▪ Adaptive	▪ Linear ▪ Iterative ▪ Time-boxed ▪ Continuous flow	▪ Project
Throughput	▪ Traditional ▪ Adaptive	▪ Linear ▪ Iterative ▪ Time-boxed ▪ Continuous flow	▪ Project ▪ Ongoing
Cumulative flow	▪ Traditional ▪ Adaptive	▪ Linear ▪ Iterative ▪ Time-boxed ▪ Continuous flow	▪ Project ▪ Ongoing
Earned schedule	(Not advised)		
Takt time	(Not advised)		

2.1   *Metric: Percentage of scope complete*

Question(s) answered
- Are we on track to complete the planned scope on schedule?
- Description
- The amount of planned work that has been completed as of the reporting date
- Value
- Early warning of potential delivery risk

Dependencies
- Approach: traditional, adaptive (with fixed scope)
- Process model: any
- Delivery mode: discrete project

Success factors
- The initial definition of 100% of scope is firm and complete.
- The budget and/or schedule may be flexible.

2.1.1   *When to use percentage of scope complete*

When scope is fixed in advance, you can use percentage of scope complete to date to gauge performance to plan. Regardless of whether you're using a traditional or an adaptive approach, and regardless of what sort of process model you're using, as long as you're working to deliver a predefined scope, it's sensible to track how much of that scope you have delivered as of a given date. This gives you an early warning of possible delivery risk.

Traditional methods usually call for delivery of the complete product at the end of a release or at the end of the entire project. Work packages in plan often don't represent complete, usable subsets of functionality. Instead, the plan defines requirements artifacts, design artifacts, test artifacts, documentation artifacts, code artifacts, and other elements as separate work packages. When using a linear process model (sometimes called a *waterfall approach*), you can track the completion of interim artifacts even though no software features are usable until the end of the project. Early warning of delivery risk is important in these cases because when a delay occurs in any phase of development, there's a domino effect through subsequent phases. Typically, such delays are absorbed in the latter phases, such as the Testing phase, which leads to the introduction of defects in production and/or unpleasant surprises in getting the product into customers' hands.

Even when scope is fixed in advance, it's possible to use adaptive development methods to deliver production-ready subsets of the solution incrementally throughout the project. In these cases, you can measure the percentage of scope complete to date by tracking the delivery of production-ready subsets of functionality. Although *agile* methods were developed to support adaptive development, many organizations use those methods as a way to slice the planned work in fixed-scope, fixed-schedule development projects. Canonical agile metrics assume you're doing adaptive development. If you're using such methods in a mechanical way to support traditional development (fixed-scope, fixed-schedule), then tracking percentage of scope complete to date may provide more useful information than tracking velocity or other agile metrics. This is a common situation, and it's an example of measuring what's really happening regardless of the buzzwords with which the process is labeled.

2.1.2   *A traditional project*

The goal of this measurement is to provide an early warning when the project is trending away from expectations. By detecting this variance early, you give yourself time to do something about it.

Let's say you're managing an initiative to deliver a software solution using traditional methods. You have a work breakdown structure (WBS) and a conventional project schedule that shows milestones through the canonical systems development life cycle (SDLC) delivery stages, such as analysis, requirements specification, architecture, design, coding, testing, acceptance, deployment, documentation, and user training.

The typical way to depict the trend in delivery performance is to show a line for *expected* performance and a line for *actual* performance. When the expected and actual lines don't diverge more than the tolerance defined for your project, the work is on track. By extending a linear trend line from the actual line, you can see whether the work is trending off plan. If the gap between expected and actual performance is growing, then you know you need to take appropriate action to bring the project back on track, and/or you need to make adjustments to the plan.

Suppose your project has a total of 800 work packages in the WBS, and according to plan your team should have completed 500 of them, or 62.5%, by August 31. The team has actually completed 400 work items, or 50% of the planned scope. You can show *percentage of scope complete to date*, as illustrated in figure 2.1. If you prefer to represent progress in terms of counts rather than percentages, you can show the same information as illustrated in figure 2.2.

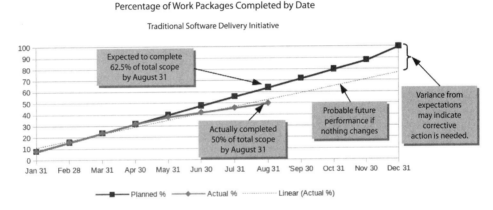

Figure 2.1   Percentage of work packages complete to date

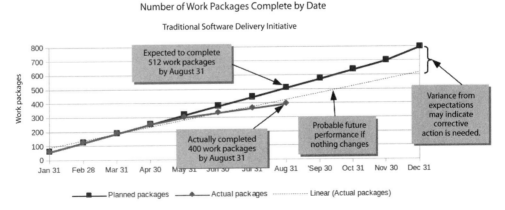

Figure 2.2   Number of work packages complete to date

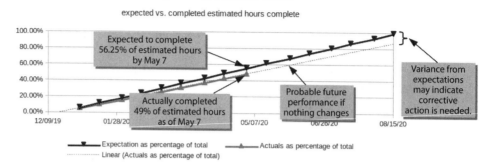

Figure 2.3   **Percentage of estimated hours complete to date**

If you prefer to show progress in terms of estimated hours, you can plot the percentage of estimated hours complete to date in the same way. Let's say your plan calls for the team to have completed 2,250 estimated hours out of a total of 4,000 estimated hours as of May 7, or 56.25% of estimated hours. The team has completed 1,960 estimated hours, or 49%. The chart looks like figure 2.3.

When you show the number of estimated hours completed compared with expectations, rather than the percentage, the chart looks like figure 2.4.

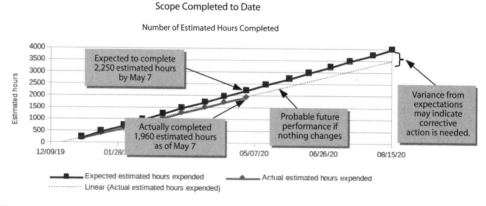

Figure 2.4   **Number of estimated hours complete to date**

Estimated or actual hours?

When using hours to compare actual performance with expected performance, be sure to use the *estimated* hours of completed tasks rather than the *actual* hours, so the units of measure for expected and actual performance are the same. Actual hours will vary from estimates, so the observed actual hours of completed tasks aren't directly comparable to the estimated hours of planned tasks.

> You might use the observed actual hours to support different metrics, namely *cycle time* and *process cycle efficiency* (described later). You might also use actual hours to help predict labor costs, if you're paying for labor on an hourly basis. If the goal is to track performance to plan, you'll want to use the estimates for completed tasks rather than the actuals.
>
> For purposes of steering work, it isn't useful to compare actual hours to estimated hours. You might do so as a way to see how accurate the estimates tend to be. This can help with process improvement, but it doesn't help with steering.

When actual performance differs from planned performance, you need to take appropriate action to steer the work. Depending on circumstances, appropriate actions may include the following:

- Change the composition of the team.
- Provide more resources to the team.
- Ask the team to work overtime on a temporary basis.
- Re-baseline the plan by changing the scope, schedule, or budget.
- Modify the plan to take reality into account.
- Cancel the project, because late delivery would reduce the anticipated return to such an extent that the project is no longer worthwhile.
- Something else.

2.1.3 An adaptive project

The goal of adaptive development is similar to the goal of traditional development (assuming scope is fixed), except that you carry out planning and tracking on a per-release basis using a rolling wave or multi-horizon planning approach. With adaptive methods, you deliver small subsets of the solution incrementally.

Adaptive development is usually supported by so-called *lightweight* management methods. These methods don't call for a comprehensive WBS, but instead use a list of features called a *product backlog*, a *master story list*, a *work queue*, or a similar name. The units of work are called *backlog items* or *user stories* instead of work packages. The different terms come from various branded process frameworks and methodologies and don't have significantly different meanings (for the narrow purpose of this book).

Assume that your team plans its work by sizing planned work items relative to each other in terms of *story points*. Let's say the team was expected to complete 70% of the planned story points by August 31, and they actually completed 50%. Showing progress as a percentage of plan, the chart looks like figure 2.5.

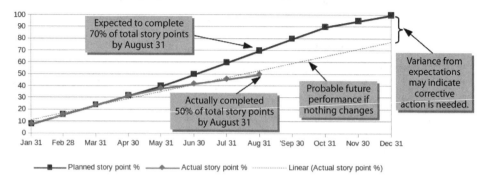

Figure 2.5   Percentage of story points complete to date

You can also show progress by comparing the total number of planned story points with the number of story points delivered. Let's say you have 1,600 story points in plan, with the expectation that the team will deliver 600 story points by May 1. The team delivers 500 story points as of May 1. The chart looks like figure 2.6.

The metric answers the same question for adaptive projects as it does for traditional ones, within the scope of a single release. When actual performance varies significantly from expected performance, you need to take corrective action to steer the work. With adaptive methods, the first choice of action is usually to adjust the plan to account for reality. But traditional corrective actions may also be appropriate, depending on circumstances and business goals.

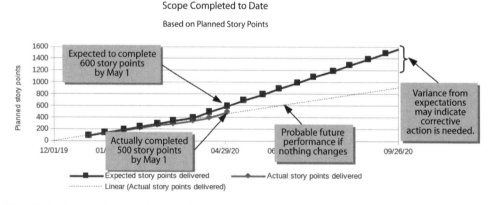

Figure 2.6   Number of story points complete to date

> ### Fixed scope required
>
> Bear in mind that this example assumes *scope* is fixed at the outset, and you're using adaptive methods to manage flexibility in *schedule* and/or *budget*. With the adaptive approach to software development, one or two of *scope, schedule,* and *budget* are fixed at the outset for business reasons, and the remaining one or two are flexible. (If people tell you all three are flexible at the same time, it suggests they don't understand the business drivers of the initiative.)
>
> You can't track percentage of scope complete to date unless the definition of *complete* is stable. So, you can use this metric with adaptive initiatives only when *scope* is fixed. When *scope* is flexible, this metric doesn't apply.

2.1.4 How to use percentage of scope complete

I've introduced *percentage of scope complete to date* by example, in the context of a couple of sample projects. You've probably gotten the gist of it, but let's cover it in a more general way just in case there are details the examples didn't make clear.

For this metric to be meaningful, a couple of key dependencies must be true. When you want to express progress in terms of a percentage toward *done*, the meaning of *100% done* has to be absolutely clear and firm. There are two implications for tracking software development work. First, 100% of scope must be clearly defined at the outset. Second, you must use the discrete project delivery mode, because the continuous-support delivery mode has no *end* by definition.

TRADITIONAL APPROACH

With the traditional approach to software development, each new software release is delivered as a discrete project, and 100% of scope, schedule, and budget are defined at the outset of the project. Therefore, the percentage of scope complete to date is always meaningful for traditional software development.

The basic planning artifact for traditional development is the *work breakdown structure* (WBS). A WBS defines *deliverables* and *work packages* that must be completed to produce those deliverables. Each work package is estimated in terms of work hours.

The definition of *100% of scope* is the sum of the estimated hours for all the work packages in the WBS. The percentage of scope complete to date is the sum of the *estimated* hours (not the *actual* hours) for all work packages that have been completed.

Any single observation of this measurement is a *trailing indicator* of delivery performance. To build a *leading indicator* to forecast future delivery performance, you plot an ideal line based on the WBS and an actual line based on the estimated hours of all completed tasks. This is illustrated in the previous examples as well as in the spreadsheet that accompanies the book. When the lines diverge, you're trending off plan.

This is a *backward-facing* metric, because the definition of success is based on your understanding of scope at a point in time in the past—the time the WBS was elaborated. Success means sticking to the original plan or the latest re-baselined plan.

What's a story point?

Throughout the book, I've been tossing buzzwords around as if everyone ought to know what they mean. That's because the book is only about metrics and isn't meant to explain every aspect of every software development methodology. I expect you to pick and choose the metrics that are relevant in your own context, based on the three factors of development approach, process model, and delivery mode. But the term *story points* seems to cause a fair amount of confusion, so let's discuss it briefly.

When contemporary lightweight development methods were first being elaborated, one of the historical problems people wanted to address was the unreliability of task-level, time-based, subjective estimation as a planning tool. One alternative to this sort of estimation is called *relative sizing*. It means development teams make a quick judgment of the *size* of each work item relative to other work items in the team's work flow. That's the key aspect of points: the size of a work item is relative to other work items, not to any specific number of hours or days.

Teams judge the size of each work item in plan without spending much time on analysis or discussion; it's a quick, gut-feel estimate. Teams usually come up with roughly similar estimated sizes, unless team members have radically different understandings about what a work item means. In that case, the sizing exercise leads to useful clarifying discussions. The exact numbers that come from the exercise aren't terribly important.

Size doesn't sound very precise, and it sounds less so when it isn't based on much analysis, and still less so when a *point* has no direct connection with time. So, how do teams arrive at sizes? They consider the anticipated level of effort for completing the task. Level of effort, in turn, may be a function of complexity, tediousness, familiarity, access to external resources, and any other relevant factors. You're then expected to *observe* the average length of time the team takes to complete stories of any given relative size. Based on those empirical observations, you can forecast the team's near-term future performance without making guesses about how long each work item will take.

But why are the points called *story* points rather than something else, like *effort points* or *coffee points*? The historical reason is that the notion of story points came about as part of the definition of *user stories*, a way of describing software functionality to be built. In methodologies that call for user stories, the relative size of the stories is expressed in terms of story points. Today, the same general approach is used with any methodology, and people often speak of the relative sizes of work items in terms of points that have no particular unit of measure.

Sometimes the points are correlated with time formulaically; for instance, 1 point might equate to 4 hours. This wasn't the original intent of story points, but many teams use them that way because it's proven difficult to break the habit of guessing at task completion times in terms of hours. When people first hear about story points, the only way they can relate to the concept is by correlating the points with time.

In your organization, people may or may not use the term *story points*. If they do, then they may or may not use story points in the way they're meant to be used. This makes no difference for measurement. Your task is to recognize how the work flows in your organization and to measure what is actually happening, regardless of the way people label things.

ADAPTIVE APPROACH

With the adaptive approach, one or two of scope, schedule, and budget are flexible by design. There may be hard limits that can't be exceeded without negating the return on investment, but the initial definitions aren't considered to be set in stone. Percentage of scope complete to date is meaningful for adaptive development *only* when the scope is fixed at the outset and when the work is carried out as a discrete project.

The basic planning artifact for adaptive development is a high-level list of business capabilities that has been partially decomposed into software features and, possibly, architectural setup tasks. Depending on the process framework in use, this may be called a *product backlog*, a *work queue*, a *master story list*, or a similar name. To keep things simple, I'll use the term *product backlog* (probably the most widely used term as this is written).

Only enough up-front analysis and design is carried out to identify major risks and to set a general direction for development. The items listed in the product backlog are far less detailed than those in a traditional WBS. Therefore, the estimates have a higher degree of uncertainty. This is normal for adaptive development, because the intent is to discover and evolve the details as you progress.

With the adaptive approach, features may be estimated in terms of time, or *sized* relative to one another using a point system, with no reference to time. In some organizations, people relate the points to time formulaically; for instance, they might say that it takes two days to deliver 10 points. This isn't the proper way to use relative sizing, but you may have to deal with it in your organization. If this is the situation in your case, then use the estimated time (and not the points) to track percentage of scope complete. It's in effect a traditional project posing as an adaptive one, so you want to use measures that correspond with the way the work is really being done.

The definition of *100% of scope* is the sum of all the high-level estimates (usually in days, because you're working with high-level feature descriptions) or sizes (in points) for features initially planned in the solution. The percentage of scope complete to date is determined by summing the estimates (not the actuals) for all backlog items that have been completed.

Any single observation of this measurement is a *trailing indicator* of delivery performance. To build a *leading indicator* to forecast future delivery performance, you plot an ideal line based on the product backlog and an actual line based on the estimates or points of all completed backlog items. This is illustrated in the previous examples as well as in the spreadsheet that accompanies the book. When the lines diverge, you're trending off plan.

This is a *backward-facing* metric, because the definition of success is based on your understanding of scope at a point in time in the past—the time the product backlog was elaborated. Success means delivering the fixed scope that was initially defined.

2.1.5 Anti-patterns

Any metric can be misused. Here are some common misapplications of percentage of scope complete, also known as *anti-patterns*.

THE EASY RIDER

Managers or teams cherry-pick the easy bits of traditional methods and the easy bits of adaptive methods in a misguided attempt to avoid the more challenging aspects of software delivery. They have neither a reliable definition of 100% of scope nor any robust mechanisms to adapt schedule and budget to manage variable scope. The typical pattern is that stakeholders assume the initial statement of scope represents a hard-and-firm commitment on the part of the delivery organization, although it's only a high-level summary of desired features. The outcome is both predictable and avoidable—cost and schedule overruns—and yet the pattern is repeated frequently. Someone, somewhere, is doing it right now. They won't see the anvil that is plummeting toward them until it's too late to take corrective action.

IT'S ONLY A REWRITE

When the purpose of the initiative is to replace an existing solution with a new one that has the same features but is based on a newer set of technologies, planners assume there's no need to investigate the functional requirements for the replacement solution. After all, "everyone" already knows what the old system does. There's no need to write any of it down. All the delivery team has to do is implement the current feature set with the new technologies. How hard could *that* be? To save costs, you can staff the project with temporary contract programmers who have never seen the old system. While you're at it, you can throw in a few new features, too. You just have to expect significant cost and schedule overruns.

THE NOVICE TEAM

When managers or teams first begin to apply adaptive development methods, they sometimes assume traditional practices such as in-depth requirements analysis or up-front design are obsolete and unnecessary regardless of context. When the context of the adaptive initiative is that scope is fixed, you need a comprehensive definition of the work items that must be completed. It isn't meaningful to track percentage complete when the definition of 100% is variable.

2.2 Metric: Earned value

Question(s) answered
- Are we on track to complete the planned scope on schedule and within the allocated budget?

Description
- The amount of budgeted cost that has been used up as of the reporting date
- Value
- Early warning of potential cost and/or schedule variance

Dependencies
- Approach: traditional
- Process model: any
- Delivery mode: discrete project

Success factors
- The initial definition of 100% of scope, schedule, and budget are firm and complete.

2.2.1 When to use earned value

Earned value (EV) has been around a long time. It's well documented and widely used. Many managers believe it's the best or only way to track progress. Yet EV depends on having the full scope defined in advance, the delivery schedule fixed in advance, and the full budget allocation defined in advance. When one or more of these factors is variable, the input values for EV formulas change throughout the project, causing the results to be useless for their intended purpose. For that reason, EV shouldn't be used with adaptive development.

EV is commonly used in very large-scale programs that involve other activities besides software development and that may involve hundreds or even thousands of subcontractors, each working on a small piece of the puzzle. Under those circumstances, software development teams don't have direct access to customers. They work to a set of specifications for their piece of the work only. Possibly the only way they can get a sense of the "value" of their work is to consider the budgeted cost of each work package in plan, and treat that cost as a value.

That said, it's possible to use a subset of EV formulas and to simplify those formulas to whatever extent makes sense in context. The EV literature doesn't require the highest degree of formality for every project. EV can be tailored to circumstances. I've heard percentage of scope complete to date described as a very basic version of EV. But EV can't be tailored to handle adaptive development, because it assumes the full scope, schedule, and budget are set in advance and the budgeted cost of each work package is known at the outset.

2.2.2 A traditional project

Let's say you're managing a traditional software development project and you want to know how well the work is proceeding as compared with the project plan. You begin work with scope fully defined, including a work breakdown structure (WBS) that includes estimated hours and budgeted cost per work item.

What's a work package?

With this sort of planning, the work items in plan are usually called *work packages* or *deliverables*. In your organization, people may use terms like these, or they may label the work items using a more contemporary term like *user story* or *minimum marketable feature*. Because the work is done using traditional methods, the more popular contemporary terminology doesn't change anything substantively. This is one reason you must pay more attention to the way work is actually done than to the way things are labeled.

Typically, the cost of a work package is based on the hourly labor rates for the types of work involved in completing the work package multiplied by the estimated number of hours to complete the work package.

For example, assume that one of the work packages (let's call it Calculate Sales Tax) involves an estimated 4 hours of analysis, 10 hours of programming, and 4 hours of testing. Furthermore, assume that in your company the average fully burdened hourly rate for a business analyst is $50, for

Budgeted cost of work package "Calculate Sales Tax"	
Business Analyst hourly rate	$50
Programmer hourly rate	$75
Software Tester hourly rate	$60
Estimated hours for analysis	4
Estimated hours for programming	10
Estimated hours for testing	4
Cost of analysis	$50 x 4 hours = $200
Cost of programming	$75 x 10 hours = $750
Cost of testing	$60 x 4 hours = $240
Budgeted cost	$1,190

Figure 2.7   Budgeted cost of a work package

a programmer it's $75, and for a tester it's $60. The budgeted cost for the work package is shown in figure 2.7.

To use EV effectively, you need to know the budgeted cost of every work package in scope before beginning development. This gives you the basis for projecting future budget performance and schedule performance so you can get an early warning about any potential delivery risks.

EV uses a few data points and a handful of simple equations to calculate *cost variance* (CV) and *schedule variance* (SV) as of a given reporting date. Here are the basic terms and equations:

- *Planned value* (PV), also known as *budgeted cost of work scheduled* (BCWS), is determined by multiplying the estimated hours by the hourly labor rate(s) for the work in scope, as shown in figure 2.7. You do the same for all the work packages in the WBS to arrive at the overall PV for the project.
- *Earned value* (EV), also known as *budgeted cost of work performed* (BCWP), is determined by multiplying the percentage of work complete to date by the total project budget.
- *Actual cost* (AC), also known as *actual cost of work performed* (ACWP), is the observed actual spend as of the reporting date.

Using EV as the base, you can calculate the CV and SV as of the reporting date to get an idea of whether the project is likely to come in on schedule and budget. The calculations are as follows:

- CV = EV − AC
- SV = EV − PV

For example, assume that your project is planned for 10 months with a budget of $1,000,000. You're partway through the project, and the numbers are as shown in figure 2.8.

Negative CV means the project is trending over budget.

Date	Planned % Complete	PV (BCWS)	Actual % Complete	EV (BCWP)	AC (ACWP)	CV = EV − AC	SV = EV − PV
07/01/20	10%	$100,000.00	8%	$80,000.00	$120,000.00	-$40,000.00	-$20,000.00
08/01/20	20%	$200,000.00	16%	$160,000.00	$240,000.00	-$80,000.00	-$40,000.00
09/01/20	30%	$300,000.00	24%	$240,000.00	$360,000.00	-$120,000.00	-$60,000.00
10/01/20	40%	$400,000.00	32%	$320,000.00	$480,000.00	-$160,000.00	-$80,000.00
11/01/20	50%	$500,000.00	40%	$400,000.00	$600,000.00	-$200,000.00	-$100,000.00
12/01/20	60%	$600,000.00					
01/01/21	70%	$700,000.00					
02/01/21	80%	$800,000.00					
03/01/21	90%	$900,000.00					
04/01/21	100%	$1,000,000.00					

Negative SV means the project is trending over schedule.

Figure 2.8   Raw data for EV

For a visual representation of the status, it's useful to show AC, PV, and EV, as in figure 2.9. The gap between EV and AC shows the CV, and the gap between EV and PV shows the SV. The unit of measure is currency, because the calculations are based on the project budget.

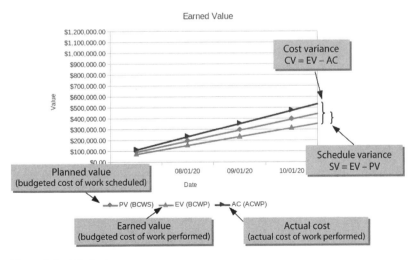

Figure 2.9   EV chart

2.2.3 Anti-pattern: the novice team

People slip into anti-patterns when they misunderstand the dependencies for using EV or when they assume traditional measurements will work properly with adaptive methods.

EV works well when you want to track project performance against a comprehensive plan. Like any comparison of current progress against a 100% standard, EV works when the definition of 100% remains stable. When you begin development with a firm definition of 100% of scope and budget and a hard-and-fast delivery date, you can use EV to track performance to plan.

This implies *big design up front* (BDUF), a firm completion date, and a complete budget allocation at the outset of the project. With adaptive methods, scope may be loosely defined, the schedule may be flexible, and an incremental funding model may be used.

The most common anti-pattern for using EV occurs in organizations (or with project managers) that are new to adaptive methods. The error is to apply traditional measurements such as EV in the context of adaptive development. With adaptive methods, you begin development without a comprehensive definition of all three of scope, schedule, and budget. The basis of EV is to compare expected performance to date against actual performance to date. Because scope, schedule, and/or budget are subject to frequent change during an adaptive development project, there is no stable definition of 100% for any of these elements. Lacking a stable definition of 100%, it isn't meaningful to express the current status as percentage complete to date.

2.3 Metric: Budget burn

Question(s) answered
- Do we have enough money to complete the planned work on schedule?

Description
- Predicted budget performance based on actual spending to date
- Value
- Warning of potential cost overrun

Dependencies
- Approach: any
- Process model: any
- Delivery mode: discrete project

Success factors
- The total budget for the project or for a distinct phase or release is allocated in advance— that is, any sort of funding model other than a recurring expense budget.

2.3.1 When to use budget burn

Once resources have been obtained and teams are organized, the cost of software development work is usually a fixed, recurring cost. Unless you have no financial concerns at all, it's useful to track the rate at which you're using up the funds for the work. This is true whether you have a fixed budget allocation or you're using some form of incremental funding. With traditional methods, you can get an early warning that you'll run out of funds before the schedule has run its course. With adaptive methods, you can see whether there will be sufficient funding to meet development goals based on teams' forecast delivery performance. With incremental funding, tracking the rate at which funds are used helps inform business decisions about whether to continue development, shift gears, or cancel the work before too much money has been invested. Whatever the model, money is money and time is time.

2.3.2 A traditional project

Assume you're responsible for a traditional software development project in which scope, schedule, and budget are all fixed in advance. One of the key questions you must be able to answer at all times during the project is, "Will we run out of money before we run out of time?" A simple way to answer this question is to compare the planned outlay with the actual outlay to date.

Suppose you're partway into the project, and your numbers look like those shown in figure 2.10. You can see from the numbers that you've spent more than you expected as of November 1, 2020. A visual comparison of actual versus expected spend makes it clear whether you're likely to run out of money by the end of the project. Figure 2.11 provides a line chart showing monetary amounts.

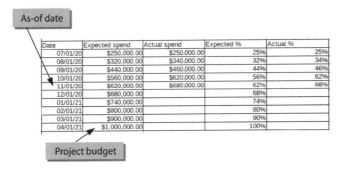

Figure 2.10 Raw data for the budget burn metric

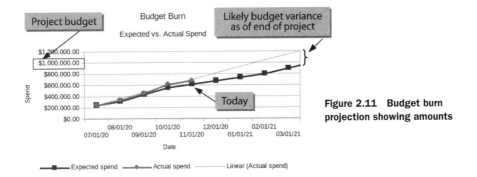

Figure 2.11 Budget burn projection showing amounts

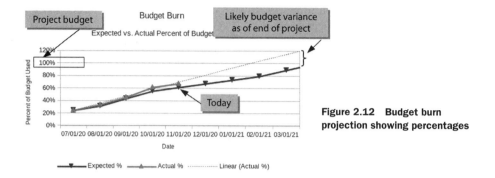

Figure 2.12   Budget burn projection showing percentages

The gap between the expected spend and the linear trend line from actual spend shows the likely budget variance as of the planned end date of the project. The same information can be shown using percentages, as you can see in figure 2.12.

2.3.3   *An adaptive project using beyond budgeting*

Funding of adaptive projects can take different forms. Many projects are started with a fixed budget allocation even if they use adaptive methods during execution. Others are funded on an as-needed basis with a cap or not-to-exceed (NTE) limit on total costs. Some use set-based concurrent engineering (SBCE) to explore alternative solutions up to a point, after which funding is funneled into the selected solution. Some run a proof-of-concept phase initially and decide whether and how to proceed with the full solution based on the results of the proof of concept. Some take a *lean startup* approach to product development, vetting proposed application features by placing a rudimentary implementation into the hands of a select group of real customers to obtain their feedback and adjusting plans accordingly. Some use the *beyond budgeting* approach across the portfolio, revisiting risks and business priorities on a periodic basis and adjusting the course and funding of all in-flight initiatives accordingly. In any case, tracking the budget burn is always helpful in steering a project.

When funds are allocated more than once in the course of a project, you want to track the budget burn for each period of time in which funds are provided. Let's say you're managing a project in a company that uses beyond budgeting. On a quarterly basis, senior management revisits their assumptions, priorities, risks, and return on investment calculations. They assess competitor actions, customer feedback, operating costs, market trends, regulatory changes, technological advances, currency fluctuations, and other factors. Your project, along with every other project in the portfolio, may be canceled, increased or reduced in scope, raised or lowered in priority, or redirected toward a different goal. You receive funding for three months at a time. For each three-month period, you want to track the budget burn to be sure you can complete the work planned for the quarter.

The numbers shown in figure 2.13 tell you that you'll run out of funds before the end of the first quarter unless something changes. Given the assumptions underlying this example, you can probably request additional funding to see you through the

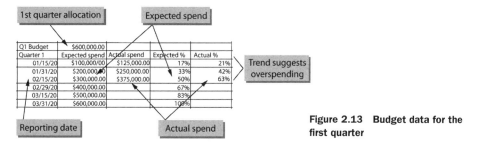

Figure 2.13   Budget data for the first quarter

quarter. Remember that the company uses beyond budgeting, which means there are funds available that can be shifted around as priorities and realities change. All the money isn't locked down in up-front budget allocations. In addition, the company isn't encumbered with tedious and politically risky change procedures. Besides that, your project has a relatively high priority in the portfolio for this quarter, so it will receive preferential treatment compared with most other in-flight initiatives. By using this metric to get an early warning about a potential cost overrun, you can make appropriate adjustments while it's still cost-effective to do so.

You can chart this based on actual amounts or percentages, as shown in figures 2.14 and 2.15. Whether you examine the spreadsheet, the chart showing amounts, or the chart showing percentages, the numbers tell you that you'll spend more than expected by the end of the quarter unless something changes. In this case, the variance is negative (insufficient funds are allocated). Positive variance is also possible. Let's proceed to the second quarter to see how that would look.

Assume that senior management has made some adjustments to the strategy for the second quarter. A competitor has introduced an attractive option to customers, and you want to match it quickly to avoid losing market share. In addition, the government in one of the countries where you operate has changed regulatory rules that affect your business, and you must make software changes to support the new rules. These initiatives take precedence over your project, which now has a lower priority than before. Your team is reduced in size from 20 people to 12 to support the two high-priority initiatives. Accordingly, your funding for the second quarter will be

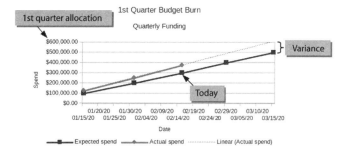

Figure 2.14   Budget burn by amounts for the first quarter

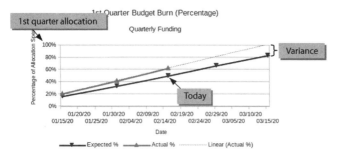

Figure 2.15   Budget burn by percentages for the first quarter

$400,000 instead of $600,000. Of course, the scope you're expected to deliver is smaller, as well.

In the second quarter, you find you're able to complete your work faster than expected. Midway through the quarter, your budget burn numbers tell you you're performing better than expected, as shown in figure 2.16.

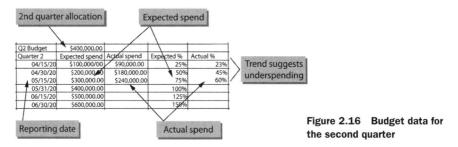

Figure 2.16   Budget data for the second quarter

The improved performance may be due to various factors. Perhaps the reduced scope of work proved to be simpler than the original scope. Perhaps the smaller team is spending proportionally less time achieving clear communication among themselves than the larger team could achieve. Perhaps the team implemented process improvements that streamlined the work flow. Whatever the reasons, you're likely to complete your work for the second quarter with money left over. This information enables planners to make decisions that enhance the organization's overall performance, possibly by shifting some of the unneeded funds to one of the high-priority initiatives.

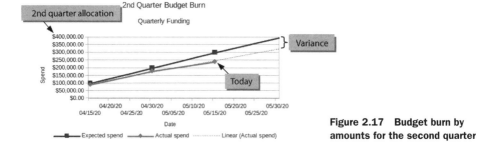

Figure 2.17   Budget burn by amounts for the second quarter

As before, you can chart the budget burn using actual amounts or percentages, as shown in figures 2.17 and 2.18. This time, the budget variance is positive. You can see this because the actual spend is trending below the expected spend.

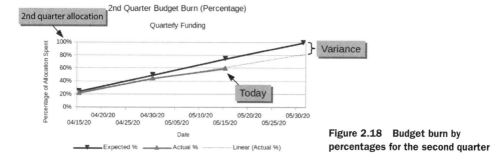

Figure 2.18 Budget burn by percentages for the second quarter

Now, let's say your project is once again a priority for the company in the third quarter. You have $720,000 and the original team of 20 at your disposal to complete the work. Midway through the quarter, your spend looks like that shown in figure 2.19.

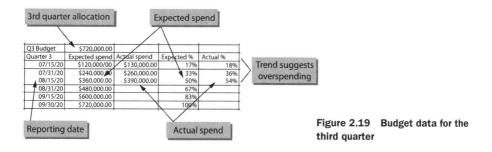

Figure 2.19 Budget data for the third quarter

The numbers indicate that you're likely to need a little more money than anticipated, but the variance is smaller than in the first quarter. Based on this, it might be premature to shift funding from lower-priority initiatives into your project, but the spend will be something to pay attention to over the next two or three weeks. That's the sort of business decision you can make to steer the project based on this metric.

As always, you can chart this data using the actual amounts or percentages, as shown in figures 2.20 and 2.21.

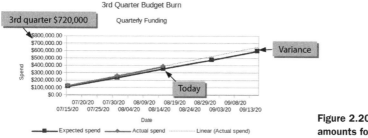

Figure 2.20 Budget burn by amounts for the third quarter

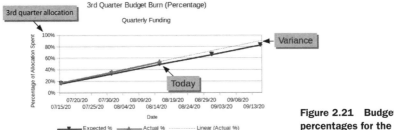

Figure 2.21   Budget burn by percentages for the third quarter

2.3.4   *Anti-pattern: agile blindness*

Fiduciary management is a fundamental part of managing any initiative, but in the past decade or so, teams have often neglected to track their budget burn when they use "lightweight" management methods.

The popular agile approach to software development has proven to be very useful when time to market is a key business driver or when there's high uncertainty about the final shape of the solution necessary to support a business vision. The most widely used methods associated with this approach are silent on the subject of fiduciary management. They focus instead on how to keep the work flowing smoothly and how to achieve flexibility in the face of changing needs. Although these are important aspects of agile development, you still have to keep in mind other necessary functions of project management.

Sometimes managers and teams forget to apply what they already know about managing projects when they first apply agile methods. In their enthusiasm to "be agile," they lose track of where the money's going. They can be blindsided by unexpected cost overruns that cripple their projects.

2.4   *Metric: Buffer burn rate*

Question(s) answered
- Will we exceed our planning buffer before we run out of time?

Description
- Monitor the burn rate of the planning buffer.
- Look for trends that indicate emerging delivery risks.

Value
- Early warning of potential delivery risks
- Dependencies
- Approach: any
- Process model: any
- Delivery mode: discrete project

Success factors
- No special success factors

2.4.1 *When to use buffer burn rate*

It's a common practice to define a *planning buffer* when planning a project. But regardless of how carefully you analyze and plan, there are always unknowns to be discovered along the way. One way of coping with this reality is to leave some room in the plan for delay, experimentation, and expanded scope.

For traditional projects, the conventional rule of thumb is to plan a 35% buffer in the schedule. Depending on context, it may be feasible to define a smaller buffer than that. For instance, if an organization typically carries out many projects of a similar nature in a familiar environment, then there may be fewer unknown issues. Another factor is estimation confidence. People who have significant experience in a particular domain may be highly confident about their estimates and feel they don't need a large planning buffer. I've seen planning buffers as small as 5% and as large as 50% for traditional software development projects.

For adaptive projects, development begins on the basis of a high-level vision for the future state. There isn't a comprehensive project plan with all the details spelled out. Yet in nearly every case, there is an upper bound on the schedule and a practical limit on spending for the project (usually called *not to exceed* [NTE]). To get a realistic sense of the timeline, the conventional rule of thumb is to plan a 100% buffer for adaptive projects. That is, if the entire future state vision is implemented, it's likely to amount to about double the amount of work that you can identify at the start of the project. As with traditional projects, the variation differs by context.

2.4.2 *How to use buffer burn rate*

The first step is to define the planning buffer for the project. If the buffer is exceeded, it means the project has overrun its budget or timeline. You've seen that you can anticipate budget and schedule overruns by monitoring the difference between planned performance and forecast actual performance, using percentage of scope complete to date or a burn chart based on observed velocity (described later in this chapter). An alternative is to monitor the consumption of the planning buffer. The typical way to chart this is with a *fever chart*, as in figure 2.22.

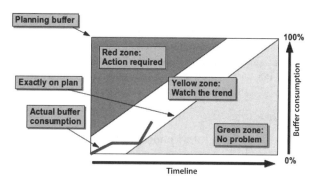

Figure 2.22 Buffer burn rate fever chart

A fever chart tracks a variable to show when its value goes outside of defined boundaries. It depicts three regions, usually called Green, Yellow, and Red. If the variable remains in the Green zone, there's no problem. If it goes into the Yellow zone, you need to pay attention and deal with any emerging delivery risks. If the variable goes into the Red zone, the project is in trouble.

To set up a fever chart, define the upper bound of the Green zone as the base project plan with no buffer. Define the lower bound of the Red zone as the project buffer. The Yellow zone gives you a safety margin between performance to plan and high delivery risk; define its bounds at some reasonable level below the project buffer.

The purpose of a fever chart is to trigger action when a variable takes on a value outside of normal bounds. The variable in this case is planning buffer consumption. If your buffer is 50%, then you'll want to set the Yellow zone at a point below 50% that gives you an opportunity to take corrective action before the project gets into trouble. It could be, say, 20% or 25%.

2.5   *Metric: Running tested features*

Question(s) answered
- How many of the planned features of the solution are in a production-ready state?
- Are we creating regressions (breaking previously working code) as we deploy new features?
- Are we likely to complete sufficient functionality on schedule to provide enough business value to justify continuing the project?
- How much time will we need to complete a given set of features for the new solution?

Description
- A simple count of the software features that have been or could be deployed to production. It's a forward-facing metric.

Value
- Provides a mechanism to track progress toward the project goal when there's no firm definition of 100% of scope

Dependencies
- Approach: adaptive
- Process model: iterative, time-boxed, or continuous flow
- Delivery mode: discrete project

Success factors
- Throughout development, the team delivers subsets of the solution incrementally to a target environment where the features are exercised regularly using automated tests.
- The team uses automated test cases at multiple levels of abstraction to ensure that the features complete to date are functioning properly and that updates to the code base haven't broken previously working features.

2.5.1   *When to use running tested features*

Running tested features (RTF) is meaningful whenever you're delivering production-ready increments of the solution throughout the development effort. Incremental delivery is the norm with adaptive development. When agile methods are used to support a traditional development project, features may be delivered incrementally as well. In either of these cases, RTF can be used to show progress toward delivery goals.

2.5.2 An adaptive project

Let's say you're responsible for an adaptive software development project. At the start, the general business vision is clear, but the details of the solution are uncertain. Using the adaptive approach, your team will explore the solution space in collaboration with key stakeholders until they have delivered sufficient business value to declare victory and move on to another project.

This sort of project doesn't have a firm definition of 100% of scope or any detailed analysis and design of solution components as of the start of development. For those reasons, you can't use backward-facing metrics that compare actual performance with a plan created in the past. Instead, you need forward-facing metrics that provide empirical information about delivery performance so that you can predict potential delivery risks and plan the ongoing work.

RTF is a simple count of the number of software features currently deployed to a test environment with all automated test cases passing. RTF is useful in this case because it doesn't depend on a stable definition of 100% of scope. Let's say your project has been in progress for several months, and the RTF chart looks like the one shown in figure 2.23.

RTF serves an informational function as both a trailing indicator and a leading indicator. If the project began on 12/1/2019, you can see that the team first delivered a usable software feature in about a month's time. Looking across the first 8 months of development, the team sustained an average rate of delivery of about 1.75 features per

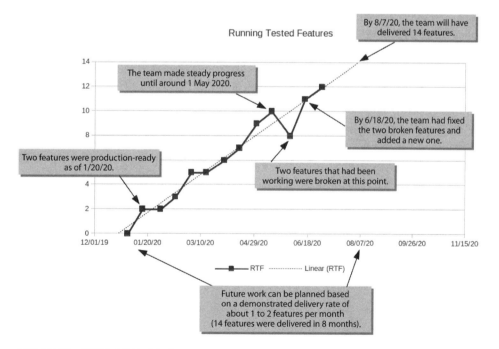

Figure 2.23   Running tested features

month. This provides a forward indicator that helps you understand how many months the team will need to complete X number of features, or how many features the team can deliver in X number of months. These numbers are approximate but reality-based, and therefore useful for planning.

The chart also shows points in the development process when the team encountered problems. This chart shows just one such event, around early May 2020. RTF serves a diagnostic function by highlighting times when the team breaks previously working code.

2.5.3   *Anti-pattern: the easy rider*

RTF is very sensitive to two key factors:

- Features must be delivered incrementally throughout development, not delivered in "big bang" fashion at the end of each release.
- The software must be exercised by automated test cases on a regular basis (at least daily).

You have seen the easy rider anti-pattern once before in this chapter. It occurs when teams try to combine the easy bits of traditional and adaptive methods while avoiding the hard bits. With respect to RTF, the easy rider anti-pattern can occur when a team isn't disciplined about two of the hard parts of adaptive methods just mentioned: regularly delivering solution increments to a target environment, and/or regularly exercising the code with automated and manual tests.

A feature isn't complete when the requirements have been specified. It's still not complete when the code has been written. The feature is complete only when the key stakeholders have accepted it as complete. This is usually based on passing acceptance tests, passing regression tests, satisfaction of nonfunctional requirements, and a successful demonstration of the feature for the key stakeholders. Any shortcuts in these areas render RTF meaningless.

2.6   *Metric: Earned business value*

Question(s) answered

- What proportion of the anticipated business value has been delivered to date?
- Have we achieved the goals of the project well enough to declare victory and move on?
- Is it worth the cost to continue developing the remaining features?
- Are we focusing on the highest-value features of the solution?

Description

- Tracks the relative amount of planned business value that has been delivered to date

Value

- Provides a mechanism to monitor business value delivery when there's no comprehensive up-front plan

Dependencies

- Approach: adaptive
- Process model: iterative, time-boxed, or continuous flow
- Delivery mode: discrete project

Success factors

- Active involvement of key stakeholder(s) with continue/terminate decision-making authority
- The relative anticipated business value of each feature is assigned by key stakeholder(s) when the feature is defined.

2.6.1 When to use earned business value

With the traditional approach, stakeholders have no option but to wait until the complete solution has been delivered before they can see whether they really need all the features that were specified in the original plan. Typically, stakeholders request every feature they can think of at the outset, because they know there will be little opportunity to make changes once the project's budget and resources have been allocated.

One of the advantages of adaptive development is that it allows stakeholders to make the decision to end development early if they've received enough value to satisfy their business needs, to free up funding and resources for other work. Adaptive development accepts the reality that no one can accurately and fully envision every detail of their future needs. What people *can* do is specify the business capabilities that the new software must support. From that point forward, the details are subject to change.

So, how can you measure the value that stakeholders have received to date throughout the course of a software development initiative? A simple and practical metric is earned business value (EBV), originally developed by Dan Rawsthorne, a thought leader in the Agile community.

2.6.2 An adaptive project

Let's say you're responsible for delivery of a project to enable two business capabilities. A set of software features has been identified that will support each capability. You have a hard due date, and you need to manage the work in a way that assures the maximum feasible business value is delivered by that date. An initial functional decomposition of the capabilities and supporting feature sets looks like figure 2.24.

In keeping with the general philosophy of adaptive development, you want to deliver the highest-value functionality of the solution early. A basic functional decomposition doesn't show you which capabilities and features are more valuable than others.

You can't use the financial value of individual features, because there's no practical way to determine their value before they've been developed. The only way to know the true value of a software feature is to offer it to the market and see what customers are willing to pay for it. That information comes too late for you to use it to steer the development work.

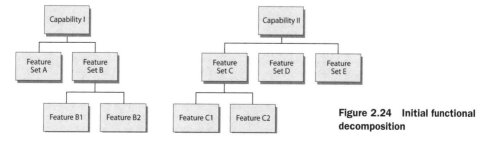

Figure 2.24 Initial functional decomposition

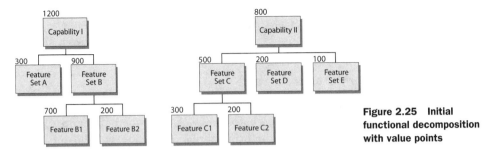

Figure 2.25 Initial functional decomposition with value points

You decide that EBV is the tool you'll use to ensure that the team delivers the highest-value features first and lower-value features as time permits. In collaboration with key business stakeholders, you assign relative business-value points to each capability, feature set, and feature in the functional decomposition. You begin with a fixed number of value points—in this case, 2,000—and allocate them across the planned features. Let's say you and your key stakeholders end up with the relative values shown in figure 2.25.

According to the key business stakeholders, Capability I accounts for 65% of the total value of the project; they assign it 1,200 of the available 2,000 value points. All the boxes under Capability I must add up to exactly 1,200 points. Feature Set B is worth 900 of those 1,200 points. All the boxes under Feature Set B must add up to exactly 900 points, and so on.

Based on this, it's clear that Capability I promises to deliver greater business value than Capability II. You can also see that Feature Set B accounts for the lion's share of the business value of Capability I. Assuming it's technically feasible, you can see that the preferred order of delivery of the planned functionality is as follows:

1 Capability I, Feature Set B, Feature B1 (35% of the value of the project)
2 Capability II, Feature Set C, Feature C1 (15% of the value of the project)
3 Capability I, Feature Set A (15% of the value of the project)

Because you're taking the adaptive approach, your understanding of the business needs and your definition of the solution will evolve throughout the project. When you add, change, and remove planned features from the project's scope, you don't change the total number of relative business points in play. As the details of the solution evolve, the total number of business value points will always total 2,000.

Going forward, you focus your efforts on Features B1 and C1. Elaborating these features further, you identify *epics* and *stories* (smaller chunks of work) that are the building blocks of the two highest-value features. The total number of points doesn't change; you must allocate fewer points to each box in the functional decomposition as you add more detail (see figure 2.26).

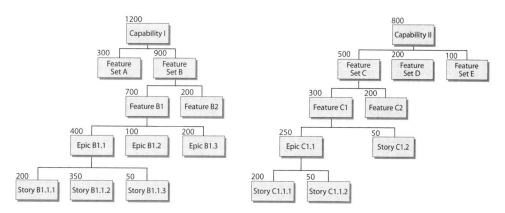

Figure 2.26   Evolving functional decomposition

You continue in the same vein as you evolve the solution. You add, remove, revalue, and split stories as you proceed with development. After some time, you reach a stage in development when the decomposition of the solution looks like figure 2.27.

The grayed-out boxes represent completed work, and the X represents a story that was dropped from scope. Notice that the overall value of the project is still 2,000 points, no matter how you shift the relative value points of the subordinate items.

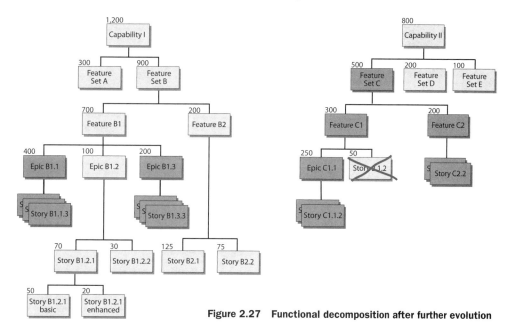

Figure 2.27   Functional decomposition after further evolution

How do you track this? Figure 2.28 shows a snippet of the spreadsheet that displays progress on these stories. When this is charted, the line representing cumulative business value delivered climbs as the team delivers the highest-value features; see figure 2.29.

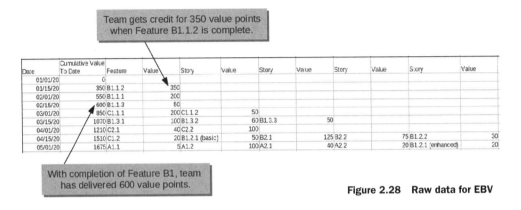

Team gets credit for 350 value points when Feature B1.1.2 is complete.

With completion of Feature B1, team has delivered 600 value points.

Date	Cumulative Value To Date	Feature	Value	Story	Value	Story	Value	Story	Value	Story	Value
01/01/20	0										
01/15/20	350	B1.1.2	350								
02/01/20	550	B1.1.1	200								
02/15/20	600	B1.1.3	50								
03/01/20	850	C1.1.1	200	C1.1.2	50						
03/15/20	1070	B1.3.1	100	B1.3.2	60	B1.3.3	50				
04/01/20	1210	C2.1	40	C2.2	100						
04/15/20	1510	C1.2	20	B1.2.1 (basic)	50	B2.1	125	B2.2	75	B1.2.2	30
05/01/20	1675	A1.1	5	A1.2	100	A2.1	40	A2.2	20	B1.2.1 (enhanced)	20

Figure 2.28   Raw data for EBV

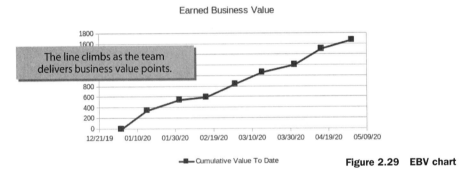

Earned Business Value

The line climbs as the team delivers business value points.

Cumulative Value To Date

Figure 2.29   EBV chart

The example shows that the team delivered high-value features in January and then lower-value features until February 19. Because they were tracking EBV, they were able to correct their course and focus on higher-value features after that.

When the team has delivered most of the high-value features, the line begins to flatten. Key business stakeholders may decide to halt the project so that the team can focus on another initiative that offers greater business value than the remaining features of the current project.

2.6.3   *Anti-patterns*

Here are some common anti-patterns in the use of earned business value.

CONFLATING BUSINESS VALUE WITH LEVEL OF EFFORT

Some teams assume that the relative difficulty of building a software feature corresponds with the relative business value of the feature. When the team has completed 50% of the work, they believe they have delivered 50% of the business value of the project. In fact, value delivered and quantity of software delivered are two completely separate considerations that have to be tracked independently.

THE ABSENTEE DECISION-MAKER

One of the assumptions in adaptive development is that key stakeholders who have decision-making authority are directly engaged with the development team throughout the project. Unfortunately, this doesn't always happen. Some teams attempt to compensate by making their best guess about the relative business value of the features in scope. This approach can result in the team delivering precisely the wrong features early on and then running out of time. It's better to dispense with tracking business value and raise the absence of a decision-maker as a potential business risk.

2.7   *Metric: Velocity*

Question(s) answered
- What is the average delivery capacity of the team per unit of time?
- Is the team delivering at a steady rate?

Description
- Empirical measurement of the quantity of work the team delivers per unit of time, for forward-facing steering

Value
- Provides a trailing indicator of variation in the team's delivery performance
- Provides data points to create leading indicators to predict the length of time the team will need to complete a given scope or the amount of scope the team can deliver in a given length of time

Dependencies
- Approach: any
- Process model: time-boxed
- Delivery mode: discrete project

Success factors
- The team completes some number of production-ready units of work per time-boxed iteration.
- The team sizes or estimates work items using a consistent scheme and scale throughout the project. This need not be (and usually isn't) comparable to the schemes and scales used by other teams.

2.7.1   *When to use velocity*

Use velocity to track a team's delivery capacity when using a time-boxed iterative process to support incremental delivery. Velocity is practical for short-term planning because it provides an empirical indicator of how much work a team can usually complete in a single time-boxed iteration. A single observation of velocity is a trailing indicator, and a series of observations can be used to populate a burn chart that provides a leading indicator of a team's likely delivery performance.

Velocity is also useful for process improvement, because it exposes irregularities in delivery performance. Once a team settles into its work flow, it should produce approximately the same amount of work in each time-boxed iteration.

When a time-boxed iterative process model is applied correctly, the team produces a production-ready solution increment in each iteration. This is one of the factors that distinguishes the time-boxed iterative model from other iterative models. Many teams attempt to use a time-boxed iterative process, but are unable to produce a production-ready solution increment in each iteration for one reason or another. Be advised that when this is the case, observations of velocity may not be meaningful.

2.7.2   *An adaptive project*

Assume you're assigned to manage an adaptive development project using a time-boxed iterative process. There's no comprehensive WBS, so you don't have a list of every task that must be completed to deliver the project, and you don't have time-based estimates on which to base expectations of delivery performance. Yet you still need to anticipate how much work the team will be able to complete in a given amount of time or the approximate amount of time the team will need to deliver a given amount of work. How can you do it?

Velocity is a metric that provides a *trailing indicator* of a team's demonstrated delivery performance. It can support either *forward-facing* tracking for adaptive initiatives or *backward-facing* tracking for traditional ones. Recent performance is a reasonably accurate predictor of near-term future performance, so a series of velocity observations can provide a *leading indicator* of a team's likely future delivery performance.

Velocity serves an *informational* function by showing a team's actual delivery performance. It serves a *diagnostic* function by highlighting irregular or erratic delivery performance. It serves a *motivational* function by providing teams with empirical feedback about their delivery performance.

Rather than time-based estimates, velocity is based on relative sizing of work items. That is, if the team feels that work item B is about twice as big as work item A, they will assign work item B twice as many points as work item A. The relative points

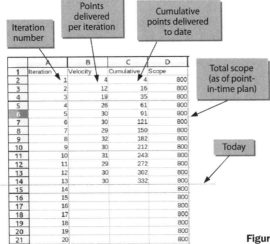

Figure 2.30   Raw data for velocity

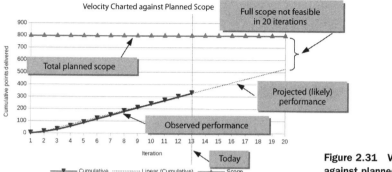

Figure 2.31   Velocity charted against planned scope

don't correspond to absolute values for estimated hours, level of effort, or similar units of measure; they have meaning only as a general indication of the relative size of work items.

A team's performance in the most recent three or four iterations gives you a pretty good idea of how they will perform in the next iteration. A trend line based on a plot of observed velocity can tell you

- How much work a team is likely to deliver in a given amount of time
- How much time a team needs to deliver a given amount of work

You can use this information to develop a forward-facing metric known as a *burn chart* to give you a leading indicator of how the work is likely to progress, assuming all variables remain unchanged. Burn charts are described later in this chapter, in section 2.9. To develop the information for velocity and burn charts, you collect observations of a team's delivery performance per iteration, as shown in figure 2.30. You can chart the information to get a visual indication of whether it's likely the team will be able to deliver the planned scope in the planned time; see figure 2.31.

Another useful way to chart the information is to show the expected completed scope to date alongside the observed performance and trend line, rather than (or along with) showing the total scope. This gives you the familiar *jaws of death* format for the line chart, as shown in figure 2.32.

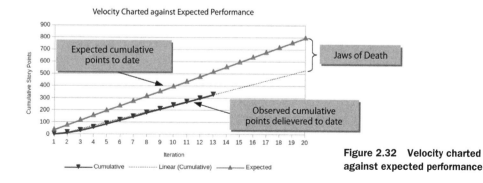

Figure 2.32   Velocity charted against expected performance

2.7.3   *Anti-patterns*

Velocity can be a useful metric in appropriate situations. It can perform an *informational* function and a *diagnostic* function when a time-boxed process model is followed properly. But velocity is easily abused. It's especially sensitive to two key elements of the time-boxed process model: maintaining a consistent iteration length, and delivering production-ready code in each iteration. In addition, velocity must be treated as an empirical observation of actual performance, and not as an estimate or target. Common errors in using velocity include the following:

- Setting targets for velocity
- Using velocity as a substitute for percentage complete
- Assuming that a team instantaneously achieves its normal velocity in the first iteration
- Assuming that a team can deliberately change its velocity to correct their schedule
- Using velocity to compare teams
- Using velocity for a mixed work flow

SETTING TARGETS FOR VELOCITY

Velocity is an *empirical observation* of a team's *actual delivery performance*. It isn't an estimate. When managers attempt to drive their teams to higher levels of performance by setting velocity targets, they risk causing an unintended *motivational* effect—teams will game the numbers to ensure that they always (appear to) meet their targets. Once that happens, velocity no longer performs the *informational* and *diagnostic* functions that help you make good decisions about the project.

I've seen many cases in which a manager attempted to coerce or trick a team into increasing their velocity, only to have the team adjust the sizes of work items in order to make their numbers while delivering the same amount of work as before. But I've also seen a counterexample—a case when a team stretched their delivery capacity by setting a velocity target. In that case, the manager met with the team to explain the strategic importance of delivering certain features by a certain date. Then the manager *asked* the team if they were willing to try to deliver at a rate that would meet that goal. The team agreed and succeeded. There were specific success factors in that case, and I don't recommend trying to aim for a velocity target as a normal practice.

That single positive example illustrates the importance of understanding—*truly* understanding—the surrounding context when selecting and using metrics. There are no hard-and-fast rules to follow mindlessly.

VELOCITY AS PERCENTAGE COMPLETE

With the adaptive approach, you don't have a comprehensive, detailed definition of 100% of scope at the outset of a project. At any given time, you have an idea of the total scope you think you'll ultimately deliver, but this is a moving target. As your understanding of the solution improves and as your design evolves, the total scope will change often.

Equating velocity with percentage complete often occurs when an adaptive project is being tracked by a manager who has a traditional mindset about scope. The manager assumes that the initial, high-level guess at the total scope is a hard-and-fast commitment. The assumption reflects a poor understanding of adaptive software development.

Another frequent cause is that higher-level management or stakeholders in the organization insist that project managers and team leads report progress in terms of percentage complete, even when the adaptive approach is used. This usually happens because people misunderstand the meaning and intent of *velocity* and assume that it's just a modern buzzword for a traditional concept. If you're required to report progress in this way, then do so; just don't assume that you can use the numbers to make critical decisions about your work.

INSTANTANEOUS MAXIMUM VELOCITY

Teams tend to settle into a performance norm once the team members get used to working together, learn about the business domain, and become comfortable with the technologies they're using to build the solution. This typically requires three or four iterations. In the first few iterations, the team's velocity will be lower than their own norm.

A common mistake on the part of project managers is to assume that a team instantaneously and automatically operates at its normal velocity from the start of a project. When the manager projects future performance on this basis, it's almost certain that the trend line will make it appear as if the project will never be completed. This leads to all sorts of uncomfortable conversations with senior management, stakeholders, and customers, when in fact there is no problem.

Figure 2.33 shows an ideal delivery projection based on the assumption that the team will achieve its normal velocity of 30 story points per iteration immediately, from the moment the project begins. This is hypothetical, of course. You can't know what the team's normal velocity will be until you observe it; the number 30 is only for purposes of illustration.

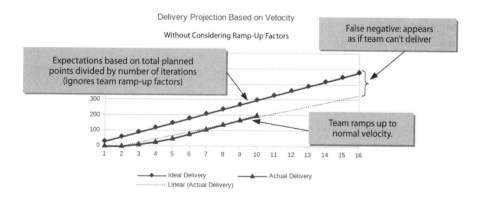

Figure 2.33 **Velocity projection assuming instantaneous maximum velocity**

Unlike a machine, a team won't operate at full speed from the instant you switch it on. It takes time for a group of people to gel into a cohesive, well-functioning team. If there's even a single new team member on board, this will have a negative impact on the team's initial velocity. In my experience, the impact of a new team is about 20% of that team's normal velocity. The impact gradually declines as the team members work out their internal pecking order and learn how to function together as a unit.

It takes time for people to get used to an unfamiliar technology set. If the team is working with different technologies than they did on their last project, or at least on a fairly recent project, then there will be another 20% impact to their initial velocity, give or take a bit. This, too, will decline gradually as the team becomes comfortable with the new technology set.

It also takes time for people to learn a new business domain. If the team is working in an unfamiliar domain, then there will be a further 20% impact to their initial velocity.

These 20% figures are rough-cut approximations based on experience with many teams. They aren't a result of any academic studies. The key is to use realistic adjustment factors to account for team ramp-up issues in the first few iterations. You know your own situation, and I don't, so use adjustments that make sense in your context. The point is this: don't assume that teams will blast out of the starting gate at full speed—not even the very best teams. They won't.

When you factor in project setup activities and account for the impact of new team members, an unfamiliar business domain, and new technologies, you can adjust the forward projection for the first few iterations and then settle into using the unadjusted actual observations once the team has ramped up to its own norm. This yields a far more realistic projection of likely future performance.

In the following example, you adjust expectations to include two iterations' worth of setup activities plus a 20% initial impact to the team's velocity for new team member integration, another 20% for new technology impact, and another 20% for new domain impact. Over the course of three iterations (3, 4, and 5), the team gradually ramps up to its own norm, which you assume to be 30 story points per iteration, for purposes of illustration. With these considerations, the projection as of iteration 2 indicates the team is on track to meet the delivery schedule. By iteration 9, the projection is confirmed using unadjusted observations of velocity, as shown in figure 2.34.

You may observe that the adjusted delivery schedule is different from the original one. The team is delivering substantially less scope in the course of 16 iterations. What can you do to recover the lost time? The answer is, nothing, for two reasons.

First, there's no lost time. The original schedule was badly planned. The original expectation was wrong because it was based on faulty assumptions about velocity. You never had the time you think you lost. Therefore, you didn't lose it.

Second, once time is lost, it's lost forever. What you've done, in keeping with the principles of adaptive development, is adjust the plan to account for reality, rather than try to force reality to comply with your original plan.

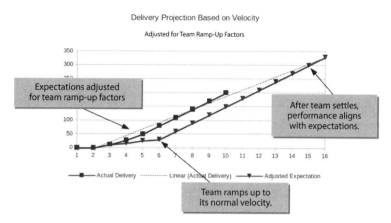

Figure 2.34   Velocity projection, adjusting for team ramp-up factors

PROJECTED PERFORMANCE BASED ON WISHFUL THINKING

When the preconditions for using velocity are in place, the metric can be useful for projecting a team's likely future delivery performance. It's good at telling you the truth about whether you'll deliver a certain scope by a given date. But it isn't so good at telling you lies so that you can feel better when your project is going off track.

I've seen cases in which project managers are unable to wrap their heads around the idea of adjusting the plan to account for reality. The only corrective action they can imagine is to make the team get back on schedule. They sometimes come up with a projection like the one shown in figure 2.35. They assert that at some point in the future, for no reason they can explain, the actual trend line will suddenly self-correct and join up with the ideal line.

What I've found most surprising is the fact that many business stakeholders and senior IT managers nod their heads gravely when a project manager presents a projection like this, as if they believe what they're looking at. Velocity is an empirical

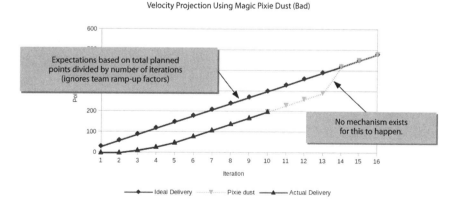

Figure 2.35   Velocity projection using magic pixie dust

measure; it's an observation of reality. There's no mechanism by which a team can abruptly quadruple its delivery capacity and then just as abruptly revert to normal. It's true that the trend line gives an early warning of potential delivery risk. It's also true that you ought to take action as early as possible to manage that risk. But this isn't effective action; it's only wishful thinking.

USING VELOCITY TO COMPARE TEAMS

It's often interesting to compare delivery teams to judge their relative effectiveness. To do this, you need to find a unit of measure that has the same meaning for all the teams. Relative points aren't such a measure. Their meaning is limited to a single team's sense of the relative size of their own work items, in their own context. Team A may have a velocity of 200 points per iteration, while Team B has a velocity of 25 points per iteration, but this doesn't imply that Team A is eight times as effective as Team B. The two teams size their work items differently.

USING VELOCITY FOR MIXED WORK FLOWS

Many teams support a set of technical assets or a suite of business applications over the long term using a *continuous support* delivery mode. The same team may also carry out *discrete projects* to implement significant enhancements to the technical environment or the applications they're supporting.

There are challenges in balancing these types of workloads. The discrete projects are probably capitalized, whereas the ongoing support work is expensed. That in itself creates an administrative burden for you. There's also a logistical challenge in that team members team can't anticipate their availability for planned work because the unplanned support work comes to them at a variable rate, and the time required to complete these work items is unpredictable.

In some organizations, teams in this situation are asked to use a *time-boxed* process model because that model works well for application development teams in other parts of the organization, and they're asked to report velocity so that all teams in the organization are using the same methods and tools. The problem is that the ongoing support work doesn't lend itself to a time-boxed process model. New work items arrive at an unplanned and irregular rate, and they may be of highly variable scope. Velocity can't be a meaningful measurement in that context.

You may have to report velocity and present your team to the outside world as using a time-boxed iterative process model in order to comply with organizational norms. Meanwhile, you must be able to answer questions about whether the work is on track. You need to have accurate early warning about potential delivery risks, even if that means tracking different metrics for your own purposes than the ones you report outward.

If your team has to handle both planned, project-style work and unplanned, support-style work at the same time, you'll find it easier to manage the work using a *continuous flow* process model. To use an empirical approach to planning, track the *cycle time* (described in the next section) of work items the same way, whether a given work item comes from a planned project or from a production support ticket. Use the mean cycle time to project the team's likely future delivery rate, in much the same way you could use velocity if you were doing a straightforward development project with no production support activities mixed in.

2.8 *Metric: Cycle time*

Question(s) answered

- What is the mean time needed to complete a single work item (possibly by category)?
- How consistent is the team's delivery performance?
- Which work items might have common characteristics that lead to delivery problems?

Description

- Projection of the team's likely future delivery performance based on empirical measurement

Value

- Provides a leading indicator of the team's delivery performance:
  - For backward-facing tracking of compliance with the plan (traditional development)
  - For forward-facing steering toward the project vision (adaptive development)
  - For capacity planning in ongoing support situations
- Can provide early warning of potential delivery risks, for either traditional or adaptive development
- Can help distinguish between common-cause variation and special-cause variation in task completion times, for purposes of process improvement

Dependencies

- Approach: any
- Process model: any
- Delivery mode: any

Success factors

- Consistent definition of the start and end of each category of work item.

2.8.1 *When to use cycle time*

Cycle time is borrowed from Lean manufacturing and adapted to software development and support work. In the context of software development, cycle time is the elapsed time from the moment a work item is started until the work item is finished.

Cycle time has the same meaning in traditional and adaptive initiatives, with any process model, and with either the discrete-project or the continuous-support delivery mode. The lack of any dependency on methods makes cycle time equally useful for steering and for process improvement. That said, cycle time isn't usually used in traditional initiatives because conventional backward-facing percentage-complete metrics provide enough information to steer such initiatives, with less effort required to collect the raw data.

2.8.2 *An adaptive project with consistently sized work items*

The simplest case for using cycle time is an adaptive development project in which the team is skilled at decomposing the work into roughly same-size chunks. Each work item represents a production-ready slice of functionality. Cycle time represents the elapsed time from the moment the team begins building a piece of functionality until that piece is deemed ready for production.

Let's say you're managing a mature, high-performing development team, and you want to use cycle time for empirically based forward planning. Because all work items are roughly the same size, you need consider only one category of work. Each work item represents a complete set of functionality, so you need not consider different cycle times for different phases or stages of work, such as analysis, coding, and testing. For those reasons, this case is the simplest example.

To collect the raw data, you note the start and end times of all work items. Over time, you calculate the mean and standard deviation of the observations. You might come up with a chart like that in figure 2.36.

You can see the raw data for this chart in the accompanying spreadsheet. It's telling you that the team has completed 25 work items so far, and the mean cycle time is about 14.7 hours. For forward planning, you can assume that the team will take approximately 14.7 hours to complete each upcoming work item.

A couple of things are worth noting. First, there's no reference to estimated task-completion times. The numbers are empirical observations of actual performance. This gives you a practical way to project future performance without having to consider variables such as *estimation optimism, perceived delivery pressure, desire to please,* or *padding to allow for unknowns,* which can affect estimates. Nor do you try to factor in external dependencies, unplanned operational problems, or other issues that can affect delivery times. You look at reality in the raw—if the team has taken an average of 14.7 hours to complete tasks in the past, then they're likely to take an average of 14.7 hours to complete tasks in the future, provided their working environment, organizational constraints, availability, and skills remain more or less the same.

Second, you're concerned with cycle times in the aggregate, and not with fine-grained differences from one work item to the next. You don't try to include outliers in calculations for future planning.

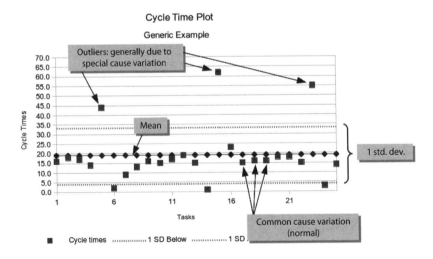

Figure 2.36 Cycle time plot

Cycle time is a measurement borrowed from the world of manufacturing. In contrast with software development, manufacturing operations emphasize consistent production of uniform widgets. A key concern is to minimize variation in the widgets produced. In software development work, each widget is a completely unique software product. When you look at variation in software development, you're concerned with variation in cycle time, not variation in the widgets you produce.

In general, variations in cycle time within one standard deviation of the mean are due to *common cause*—that is, the variation occurs because of the way the organization functions. Therefore, there's no value in chasing down the reasons for each individual variation. Variations beyond one standard deviation are usually due to *special causes*—that is, each case is a one-off situation that is unlikely to be repeated. Although these cases may be interesting for purposes of problem resolution, they don't help you with forward planning.

Based on the chart, then, you can say that if the team has 100 work items remaining in plan, and they take about 14.7 hours to complete a work item, then they will need about 1,470 hours to complete the remaining work. The result is about as accurate as you could obtain through careful estimation, and it requires far less effort.

2.8.3   *An adaptive project with variable-sized work items*

Now assume that you're managing a project in which the work items are of variable size. Broadly speaking, work items can be categorized as small, medium, or large. You can track cycle time in each of those three categories.

In figure 2.37, you see that the team has completed 12 work items deemed small. They demonstrated a mean cycle time of 5.8 hours per work item, with a standard deviation of 2.2 hours. For purposes of forward planning, you can assume that the team will continue to take about 5.8 hours on average to complete small work items.

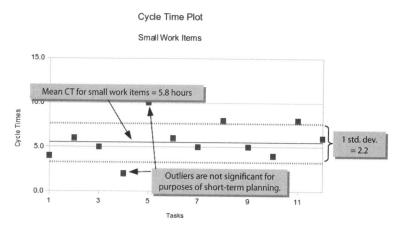

Figure 2.37   Cycle time plot: small work items

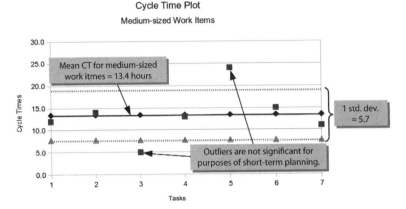

Figure 2.38   Cycle time plot: medium-sized work items

Figure 2.38 shows the team's performance in completing work items of medium size. They completed 7 medium-sized work items in a mean time of 13.7 hours.

Finally, figure 2.39 shows the chart for large work items. The team has completed 5 large work items with a mean cycle time of 25 hours.

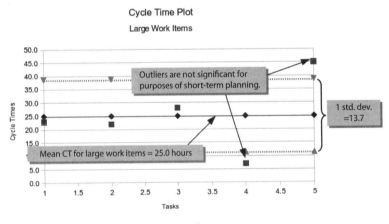

Figure 2.39   Cycle time plot: large work items

Let's say the project has 40 small, 12 medium, and 8 large work items remaining in plan. You can plan that the team will need about $(40 \times 5.8) + (12 \times 13.4) + (8 \times 25)$ hours, or $232 + 160.8 + 200 = 592.8$ hours. You can round up to 600 to get an approximate value that doesn't suggest false precision.

2.8.4   *A traditional project with phase gates*

Many traditional projects use a linear process model, sometimes called a *waterfall* model, or they wrap the conventional sequential phases in an iterative or flow-based process model. Teams deliver the complete solution all at once at the end of the project or the end of a release. They create all the requirements before writing any code, they complete all the code before beginning testing in earnest, and they complete all the testing before deploying any portion of the solution.

You might assume that cycle time can't be meaningful with this approach, because the team doesn't deliver any complete features until the end of the project, when it's too late to use metrics to steer the work. But you can use cycle time to measure the mean delivery time of interim artifacts per phase. It's an empirical measure that can give you an early warning of schedule or budget variance.

The fact that the work involved in preparing a requirements artifact is very different from the work involved in coding a module or creating a test plan doesn't invalidate cycle time. The key is to compile cycle-time observations of similar tasks in the same phase of development. Traditional projects usually take considerably more time than adaptive ones, so there's ample time in each phase for the cycle-time observations to provide useful information.

Let's say that the Requirements phase is underway, and analysts have produced requirements artifacts for the first 10 features of the solution. Per the data in the accompanying spreadsheet, you see that the analysts have taken a mean cycle time of about 14 hours to produce a requirements artifact, with cycle times between about 8 and 20 hours within one standard deviation of the mean. The cycle time plot for the Requirements phase looks like figure 2.40 (so far).

In a traditional project, the Requirements phase is only a portion of the total lead time for delivery of the solution. You might wonder about the value of predicting requirements elaboration alone, separate from the other delivery phases. The value is that you can get an early warning of potential schedule slippage or budget overruns relatively early in the project. Empirical observations of demonstrated performance provide a more accurate projection of future performance than a comparison of actual and estimated times.

You can use the same approach in each delivery phase. For example, figure 2.41 shows a plot of observed cycle times for the Coding phase. This tells you the team takes about 10 hours to complete any given unit of coding, give or take about 4.8

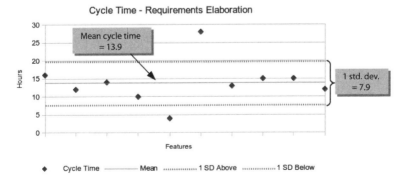

Figure 2.40   Cycle time plot: Requirements phase

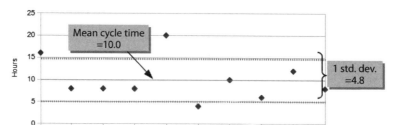

Figure 2.41   Cycle time plot: Coding phase

hours. Their performance is unlikely to change as long as other factors remain stable, such as team composition, available resources, and time stolen from the project by other tactical issues (production support, and so on).

Figure 2.42 shows a cycle time chart for the Testing phase. By this time, it's pretty late in the project schedule. Yet the Testing phase is often the time when issues that had been hidden become visible. It may appear as if everything is proceeding according to plan until you reach this phase; but now, everything that was swept under the rug or deferred in earlier phases can no longer be ignored. If you have an empirical measure you can use to predict schedule and budget performance in the Testing phase, you can determine the impact of such late discoveries before it becomes too late to take corrective action.

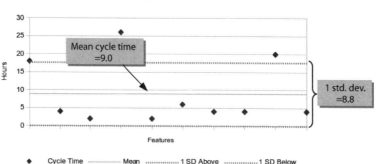

Figure 2.42   Cycle time plot: Testing phase

2.9   *Metric: Burn chart*

Question(s) answered

- Is the team likely to meet delivery targets?
- How much time will the team require to complete the planned scope?
- How much of the planned scope can the team complete by a given date?

Description

- Projection of the team's likely future delivery performance based on empirical measurement, for forward-facing or backward-facing steering

Value

- Provides a leading indicator of the team's delivery performance
- Can provide an early warning of potential delivery risks

Dependencies

- Approach: any
- Process model: any
- Delivery mode: discrete project

Success factors

- Consistent understanding of what constitutes a "work item" (by whatever name)
- Explicit, demonstrable, binary definition of what it means to declare a work item "complete"

2.9.1 When to use burn charts

Use a burn chart to develop a leading indicator of a team's likely future delivery performance based on empirical observations of their past performance. This is meaningful when the team incrementally delivers production-ready subsets of the solution, whether as part of a traditional or an adaptive development effort.

2.9.2 How to use burn charts

A *burn chart* shows the amount of work done (*burn-up chart*) or the amount of work remaining to be done (*burn-down chart*). It consists of a series of observations of past performance, an indication of planned scope, and a trend line that meets up with the planned scope at some future point.

For example, suppose the data in figure 2.43 represents observations of your team's performance to date, assuming a time-boxed iterative process model and relative sizing of work items in terms of points.

	A	B	C	D	E	F
1	Original Scope	480				
2	Iteration	Points Completed	Cumulative Points Completed	Scope (Current Plan)	Scope Change	Points Remaining
3	1	0	0	480	0	480
4	2	0	0	480	0	480
5	3	4	4	480	0	476
6	4	12	16	480	0	464
7	5	24	40	500	-20	460
8	6	26	66	500	-20	434
9	7	25	91	500	-20	409
10	8	28	119	470	10	351
11	9	26	145	470	10	325
12	10	25	170	470	10	300
13	11	25	195	470	10	275
14	12	24	219	510	-30	291
15	13	25	244	510	-30	266
16	14	26	270	510	-30	240
17	15	24	294	510	-30	216
18	16	25	319	510	-30	191
19	17			510	-30	
20	18			510	-30	
21	19			510	-30	
22	20			510	-30	
23	21			510	-30	
24	22			510	-30	
25	23			510	-30	

Figure 2.43 Raw data for burn charts

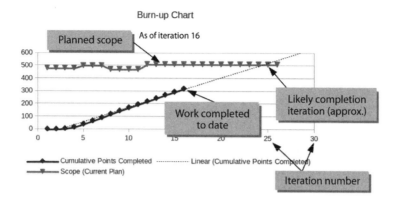

**Figure 2.44
Burn-up chart**

The points completed per iteration are the team's velocity. Individual observations of velocity are trailing indicators. To turn the observations into a leading indicator, you can show them as a burn chart. A burn-up chart shows the planned scope at the time and tracks the amount of work complete to date, as in figure 2.44.

Based on the team's actual performance to date, you can project their likely future performance to get an idea of when their output will reach the level of planned scope. When the planned scope changes, the scope line moves up or down accordingly.

The same information can be represented as a burn-down chart. This format deducts completed work from the planned scope until the work remaining reaches zero. It's the same information as in the burn-up chart, but upside-down. Many people like to see the remaining work disappear. The same data represented in the burn-up chart from figure 2.44 looks like figure 2.45 when formatted as a burn-down chart.

The zero line represents the originally planned scope. As scope changes, the scope and the target line move up or down accordingly. When the total planned scope increases, the target line dips below zero to show how far the work has to burn down in order to complete the objectives.

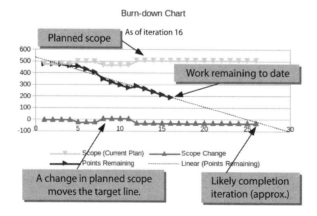

Figure 2.45   Burn-down chart

2.9.3 *Anti-patterns*

Provided you base burn charts on valid data, such as estimated task hours, velocity observations, or cycle-time observations, there isn't much you can do to corrupt them. The only problem is that people sometimes can't decide between the burn-up and burn-down forms.

MORE IS LESS

A burn chart shows exactly the same information, whether it's presented in burn-up or burn-down form. Some people like to see completed work climb toward the goal. Others like to see the remaining work progressively vanish. Either way, it's the same information.

The more-is-less anti-pattern occurs when you imagine that information will make a greater impact if it's presented in multiple forms. If you can show progress in terms of work completed as well as in terms of work remaining, isn't that twice as good as showing either one alone? Actually, it isn't. Showing the same information in two different forms on the same chart only serves to make the chart harder to understand.

If you glance at either of the burn charts shown in the previous section, you immediately perceive the progress that has been made to date and the implications for future delivery performance. If you look at the chart in figure 2.46, you have to study it a bit before you see what it's illustrating, even though it shows exactly the same information as the earlier burn-up and burn-down charts.

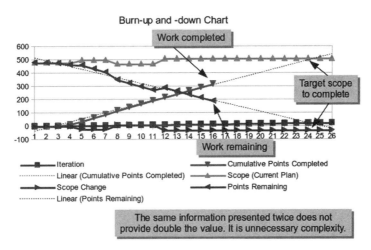

Figure 2.46 A burn-up and burn-down chart

ARTS AND CRAFTS

The arts-and-crafts anti-pattern occurs when you become enamored of the graphical capabilities of your project-tracking software. It's possible to produce charts in multiple forms, so why not create an eye-catching, colorful presentation that shows off the

Burn-up Bar Chart, Burn-down Line Chart, and Pie Chart

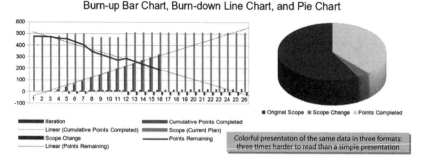

Figure 2.47   A needlessly complicated burn chart

software's charting features? Figure 2.47 shows the same information as the other charts you've seen, but in a colorful array of bar, line, and pie chart forms.

Decision-makers need clear and concise information about progress. With this sort of presentation, they must spend a certain amount of time deciphering the meaning of the charts. Any one of these formats would do the job. The three together merely reduce the signal-to-noise ratio of the chart.

2.10   *Metric: Throughput*

Question(s) answered
- How much software can the team or organization deliver in a given time?
- Does the team or organization deliver results at a consistent rate?

Description
- Empirical observation of the quantity of product delivered and available to customers per unit of time (per month, quarter, release, and so on)

Value
- Projections based on historical observations of throughput provide an accurate forecast of future delivery performance.
- If stakeholders understand the financial value of software features, they can use throughput to forecast revenue.

Dependencies
- Approach: any
- Process model: any
- Delivery mode: any

Success factors
- A realistic and honest definition of "delivered." Deployment to a staging or test environment isn't sufficient, because customers can't access the product there.
- Consistent tracking of cycle time

2.10.1   *When to use throughput*

Throughput is a metric derived from Lean manufacturing. In the manufacturing context, throughput is defined as the number of *value units* produced per unit of time. In a for-profit corporation, a value unit is typically a unit of currency and represents revenue from sales. In the context of customer support, it might refer to the number of customers assisted by the help desk each week. For other kinds of organizations, throughput can refer to some other form of value. For example, a charitable organization might track the number of meals served to homeless people per month; a government agency might track the number of tax forms processed per day.

In the context of software development, throughput refers to the number of work items completed per unit of time. The meaning of *work item* depends on the methodology you're using. It could be a work package, a user story, a minimum usable feature, or anything else that makes sense in context.

Given a continuous flow process model, you might track the number of software features delivered per month. With a time-boxed process model, throughput is the number of work items completed per iteration. This is similar to velocity, although velocity is usually based on relative sizing of work items, whereas throughput counts whole work items only. With other process models, throughput can be measured for different portions of the delivery stream, such as requirements specifications or test plans. You can track the rate of production of any type of artifact that makes sense in your situation.

2.10.2 *A mixed-model project*

Let's say you're managing a project to deliver a total of 36 work packages on a 12-month timeline. Assume that it's a traditional project in that it has a fixed scope, schedule, and budget, but your team is able to deliver increments of the solution to a production-ready state on a regular basis. This represents a mixed model that combines elements of traditional and adaptive methods and therefore doesn't lend itself easily to the metrics that are generally associated with any particular published methodology. Throughput is a useful metric in this case because it has no dependencies on approach, process model, or delivery mode.

Given a 12-month timeline starting in January and a mandate to deliver 36 work packages, your project plan generally looks like figure 2.48. To deliver 36 work packages in 12 months, the team needs to deliver 3 work packages per month on average. In other words, the team's throughput needs to be 3 work packages per month. If you plot the ideal throughput against the observed throughput from January to September, as shown in figure 2.49, it's clear that the team isn't meeting the necessary level of throughput.

Month	Work packages signed off	Average (Throughput)	Ideal throughput	cumulative delivery	Ideal cumulative delivery
Jan	0	0.00	3.00	0	3
Feb	0	0.00	3.00	0	6
Mar	2	0.67	3.00	2	9
Apr	4	1.00	3.00	6	12
May	3	0.60	3.00	9	15
Jun	3	0.50	3.00	12	18
Jul	4	0.57	3.00	16	21
Aug	2	0.25	3.00	18	24
Sep	3	0.33	3.00	21	27
Oct			3		30
Nov			3		33
Dec			3		36

Figure 2.48 Project plan

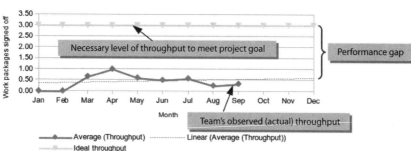

Figure 2.49   Ideal vs. observed throughput

The data through September shows that the team isn't on track to meet this goal. You want to see how long it will take the team to complete all 36 work packages, or alternatively, how many work packages they can deliver by the end of the 12-month project schedule. You can visualize this information by plotting the cumulative observed delivery to date against the ideal cumulative delivery through the planned timeline, as shown in figure 2.50.

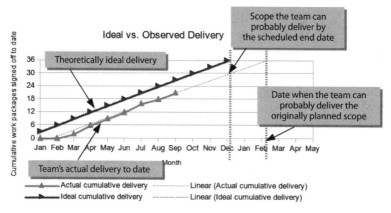

Figure 2.50   Actual vs. ideal throughput

Assuming that this team will be maintained intact across multiple projects, you can project their throughput for future projects with similar characteristics by tracking their observed delivery performance. Figure 2.51 is a chart based on the same data as the previous line charts.

Just as you did with cycle time, you discount observations that lie more than one standard deviation from the mean. You can see that the team generally delivers about one feature every two months. Unless something changes, there's no reason to expect their future performance to be any different than this.

You may have noticed something about this example that reminds you of an example from the section about velocity: the team delivered nothing in the first two months

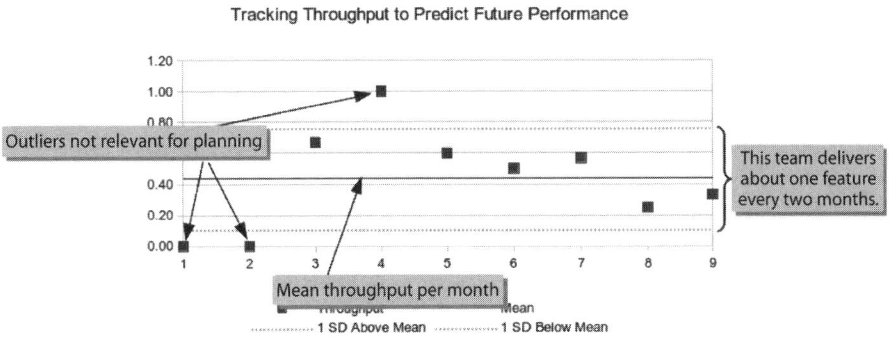

Tracking Throughput to Predict Future Performance

Figure 2.51   Using throughput to predict performance

of the project. The "ideal" throughput line assumed that they would deliver at a steady rate of three work packages per month from the beginning of the project until the end. This notion of "ideal" ignores the team's natural ramp-up time. You shouldn't have expected the team to deliver three work packages in the first month. By doing so, you set unrealistic expectations for your stakeholders.

2.11   *Metric: Cumulative flow*

Question(s) answered
- Where are the bottlenecks in the process?
- At what points do you have a buildup of work-in-process inventory (interim artifacts that represent incomplete work)?
- How deep are the queues feeding into value-add steps?
- Where are the largest components of cycle time?
- At what points is the workload unbalanced?

Description
- Visual representation of all the work done and in process to date
- Value
- Exposes delivery issues and process-improvement opportunities at a glance
- Provides direction for root-cause analysis

Dependencies
- Approach: any
- Process model: any
- Delivery mode: any

Success factors
- Queues and value-add states are identified.
- Accurate tracking of cycle time per state
- Accurate tracking of queued times

2.11.1   *When to use cumulative flow*

In a multistep delivery process, cumulative flow tracks the amount of time work remains in each step. In a rapid-delivery, collaborative process, there may be only three states for a work item: ready, in progress, and done. Even so, cumulative flow shows useful information for steering the work.

Cumulative flow exposes a number of interesting pieces of information in a visual way. These include overall throughput and throughput per step, overall cycle time and cycle time per step, queue depth, lead time, and the location of bottlenecks in the process.

2.11.2 A traditional project

Let's assume that you're tracking a traditional-style project that has the conventional waterfall steps with hand-offs between them. Although cumulative flow isn't limited to this approach to software development, and the steps need not represent hand-offs but rather stages in the evolution of features, the traditional model provides a simple example to illustrate the metric. Your project has been underway for some time, and the work has progressed through the various stages in the delivery process, as shown in figure 2.52.

Report Date	Total Scope (Features)	Requirements	Architecture / Design	Construction	Testing	Deployed
2/20/2004	100	8	0	0	0	0
2/27/2004	100	19	15	5	0	0
3/5/2004	100	30	25	12	0	0
3/12/2004	110	41	36	27	0	0
3/19/2004	110	53	49	34	7	0
3/26/2004	115	61	53	40	15	0
4/2/2004	115	74	56	48	22	0
4/9/2004	115	85	59	56	29	15
4/16/2004	125	93	62	57	40	22
4/23/2004	125	99	65	61	49	29
4/30/2004	125	106	75	70	58	40
5/7/2004	125	114	79	75	64	50
5/14/2004	125	119	88	80	68	60
5/21/2004	125	122	88	85	72	68
5/28/2004	125	122	91	90	76	72

Figure 2.52   Raw data for cumulative flow

Some people relate to the information in this form—as rows and columns of numbers. Most people, however, relate to a visualization of the information that allows interesting aspects of the team's progress to capture your attention. The previous data can be visualized as shown in figure 2.53.

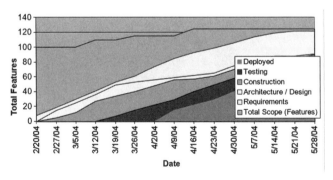

Figure 2.53   Cumulative flow diagram

This is a cumulative flow diagram (CFD). If you aren't accustomed to using CFDs, it may look like a random mass of colored smears; but once you learn to read it, a CFD speaks volumes about the status of a project.

In this example, you can see the formal steps in the delivery process for the hypothetical project: Requirements, Architecture and Design, Construction, Testing, and Deployed. Your goal is to produce the finished product—that is, to get work into the Deployed category. You want to avoid accumulating incomplete work—interim artifacts such as requirements specifications, untested code, and undeployed features.

Each filled region in the CFD represents one of the steps in your process. Ideally, work flows smoothly throughout the process, and the filled regions are about the same thickness all the way across the diagram. That's pretty rare in real life. More commonly, each step in a process has a different capacity. Steps that have high capacity generate interim artifacts more rapidly than other steps. Steps that have low capacity become bottlenecks. The CFD makes this sort of thing apparent at a glance so that you can take corrective action to keep the project on course.

Let's take another look at the CFD, in figure 2.54. It has some annotations to make it a little clearer how the diagram exposes interesting information.

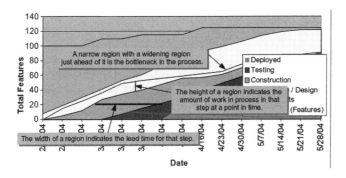

Figure 2.54   Cumulative flow diagram: annotated

You can see that Architecture and Design is the bottleneck in the process: it grows shorter while the step just ahead of it, Requirements, grows taller. You're accumulating work-in-process (WIP) inventory in the form of requirements specifications that may become stale before the team acts on them.

The amount of WIP in each step of the process at any given point in time is shown by the height of the filled regions. The average lead time per step is shown by the average width of each filled region as the work progresses. You can see the lead time for the whole process or the lead time for any sequential series of steps at a glance.

Eventually, you want to see Total Scope disappear and be entirely replaced by Deployed. Anything short of a finished product that's produced along the way represents incomplete, interim artifacts or inventory that provides no business value to stakeholders.

2.12 *Not advised*

To be pragmatic about metrics, you want to measure everything necessary to provide stakeholders with the information they need to make informed decisions to steer the work and to guide process improvements. By the same token, you want to avoid going overboard with metrics. This section mentions a few metrics that people sometimes use to track software development and delivery, but that don't help you understand how well the work is flowing or how effective your processes are.

2.12.1 *Earned schedule*

Although earned value management (EVM) is used widely in large-scale programs and provides value to planners and managers, it has a few issues that led to the creation of another metric, *earned schedule* (ES). According to www.earnedschedule.com as of May 2015,

> EVM measures schedule performance not in units of time, but rather in cost, i.e. dollars. After overcoming this mental obstacle, we later discover another quirk of EVM: at the completion of a project which is behind schedule, Schedule Variance (SV) is equal to zero, and the Schedule Performance Index (SPI) equals unity. We know the project completed late, yet the indicator values say the project has … perfect schedule performance!!

The Wikipedia article on ES as of May 2015 makes the following observations:

> Near the end of a project—when schedule performance is often a primary concern—the usefulness of traditional schedule metrics is demonstrably poor. In traditional EVM, a schedule variance (SV) of 0 or a schedule performance index (SPI) of 1 indicates that a project is exactly on schedule. However, when a project is completed, its SV is always 0 and SPI is always 1, even if the project was delivered unacceptably late. Similarly, a project can languish near completion (e.g. SPI = 0.95) and never be flagged as outside acceptable numerical tolerance.

If this critique of EV strikes you as odd, it may be due to the assertion that you're especially concerned with schedule performance *near the end* of a project. In reality, you need to know about schedule risk as early as possible in the project. The examples given in the ES literature indicate that managers discover schedule risk so late in the project that there's neither time nor money remaining to take corrective action.

It seems to me that either percentage of scope complete or EV will serve, because it will be obvious when the schedule is at risk while there's still time to do something about it. Once the project has ended, schedule risk is moot. Therefore, the fact that EV results in SV of zero and SPI of 1.0 *at the end* of a "late" project isn't a problem for steering the project, because there's no more steering to be done.

Rather than providing examples of ES, I'll suggest that this metric doesn't qualify as pragmatic for purposes of this book. If you're required to report it, then you can find descriptions of how to use it online or in other references. I don't think you should depend on ES to help you steer projects.

2.12.2 *Takt time*

Takt time is a metric adapted from Lean manufacturing. It's the rate at which widgets come off an assembly line. The basic calculation is available minutes for production / required units of production. *Available minutes* is the total amount of work time less any interruptions. *Required units* represents leveled customer demand: the rate at which customers purchase widgets.

Takt time isn't always used in Lean manufacturing. When it's used, its purpose is to match the rate of production with customer demand. This prevents finished-goods inventory from accumulating.

The theory of constraints indicates that in any multistep process, one of the steps will have lower capacity than the rest. This is known as the *constraint* (or *bottleneck*). The capacity of the constraint determines the capacity of the process as a whole.

Provided that the capacity of the constraint is greater than leveled customer demand (that is, greater than the required units of production), you can set the takt time of a manufacturing operation to match the rate of production with demand. When the capacity of the constraint is less than leveled demand, you can't produce widgets as rapidly as customers want to consume them. It's an incentive to improve the capacity of the constraint.

Lean manufacturing offers a number of useful ideas that can be applied to software development. You've already seen that you can adapt Lean metrics such as cycle time, throughput, and process cycle efficiency, and Lean practices like limiting work in process, to your work in software. Probably for that reason, some people have looked for a way to use takt time in a software-development context.

The problem is that although you can translate some concepts and measurements from manufacturing to software development, the two activities have significant differences. Takt time doesn't survive the transition from manufacturing to software development.

A manufacturing process produces identical copies of the same product again and again. A software-development process produces a single copy of each of many unique products. It isn't sensible to declare that each software product will come off the "assembly line" at a steady rate. It's a product-development process, not an assembly-line process.

Software-development organizations typically have a fixed release schedule, or they release small changes continuously. In the former case, the takt time is the same as the release schedule. In the latter case, the takt time is variable, because code is promoted to production whenever a change is made.

2.13 **Summary**

In this chapter, you learned the basic mechanics and function of several metrics that are useful for steering work in progress. More important, you learned how to correlate the characteristics of the work flow in an organization with metrics that can be meaningful and useful in different circumstances.

You learned about metrics that apply to the traditional approach to software delivery, in which risks, requirements, and costs are analyzed in detail before development begins. You also learned about metrics that apply to the adaptive approach to software delivery, in which you steer toward a general vision for the future, applying lessons learned along the way to adjust your plans and designs. In addition, you learned about metrics that are sensitive to the process model in use, and how the misapplication of these metrics can lead to meaningless numbers.

The metrics in this chapter were considered in isolation. In subsequent chapters, you'll see how multiple metrics used in concert can provide useful information both for steering and for process improvement.

Metrics for improvement

This chapter covers

- Using metrics to guide process improvement
- Metric dependencies on development, process, and delivery
- Common anti-patterns or inappropriate uses of metrics

Several of the metrics we'll cover in this chapter were described in chapter 2 in the context of steering work in progress. In this chapter, we're concerned with using the same metrics to inform process-improvement efforts. You're looking for different information from the metrics, and you'll take different actions in response to the information than in chapter 2.

3.1   Process-agnostic metrics

Delivery-performance metrics that have no dependencies on software development methods are useful for monitoring the effectiveness of process-improvement efforts because they have the same meaning regardless of how the work is carried out. On the other hand, metrics that depend on development approach, process model, or delivery mode will break if you change any of those factors as part of your improvement program. This means metrics derived from the Lean school of thought are equally useful for steering and for process improvement.

3.2 Technical metrics

In this chapter, I'll introduce two additional categories of metrics that aren't used to steer work in progress: technical metrics and human metrics. These generally aren't useful for steering, but they can be very helpful with improving a team's delivery performance. They aren't usually shared outside the team, because they're subject to misinterpretation and abuse by senior management and business stakeholders.

Technical metrics are usually extracted automatically from software build processes. They include static code analysis, performance profiling, commit history, and measurements of automated test coverage and test stability. They help teams understand where technical debt may be accumulating, identify sections of code that need attention to meet nonfunctional requirements, and uncover areas of the code base that are lacking test coverage.

3.3 Human metrics

Human metrics measure the emotional state of team members and profiles of team members' personality types and cognitive styles. These factors have become significantly more important as collaborative styles of work have gained popularity. The quality of personal interactions can have a profound effect on delivery performance as well as provide additional evidence of potential areas of improvement when combined with trends in other metrics.

3.4 General anti-patterns

We'll continue to consider anti-patterns associated with individual metrics. Two fundamental, overarching anti-patterns pertain to all measurements of performance improvement efforts: treating humans as resources and measuring practices instead of results. These are important because of the unintended motivational side effects they can have. I want to call them out before delving into the individual metrics.

3.4.1 Treating humans as resources

This may be the mother of all management anti-patterns. Management science has treated human beings as interchangeable machine parts at least since the time of Frederick Taylor's "scientific management" in the early twentieth century, and possibly much longer than that. Even today, many managers loosely refer to workers as "resources" without realizing the implications of the word.

A *resource* is an asset whose performance can be calculated and predicted with a high degree of accuracy and precision. For example, as I write this, I'm sitting in a chair. Should the chair break, I can sit in another chair. The new chair will immediately function equally as well as the old one did before it broke. The chair requires no training before it can carry out its function. It has no mood swings and never gets tired, sick, or hungry. It doesn't take vacations or need to pick up its ottoman from furniture daycare. The chair doesn't worry about other chairs from the same furniture factory that may be going through a rough patch. The new chair doesn't have a different personal style of chairness than the old chair. It doesn't interact differently with the other chairs in the room than the old chair did. It's easy to calculate the number of chairs necessary to seat 10, 100, or 1,000 people. The chair is a resource.

When team members leave, you can replace them. But the replacements won't perform at 100% capacity instantaneously. They may have general qualifications similar to those of the former team members, but not identical experience. They will each have a personal style of doing the job. They will get tired, hungry, and sick from time to time. They will take vacations and need to pick up their children from daycare. They will have hopes, fears, professional goals, mood swings, headaches, good days, and bad days. They will worry about family members and friends who may be going through a rough patch. They will have unique personality types and cognitive styles and will create a new dynamic of personal interactions on the team. It isn't straightforward to predict the impact on team performance when a team member is replaced. A team member isn't a resource. A team member is a human being.

When you measure people and predict their performance as if they were resources, it's highly likely that you'll miss important information and cause unintended behavioral side effects.

3.4.2 *Measuring practices instead of results*

When you're steering work in progress, it's pretty obvious that you want to measure outcomes rather than activity. To be able to answer questions about the status of the work, you need to know the team's general rate of delivery, the rate of financial burn, and other objective information. Tracking activity, such as the number of hours each team member spends in the office each week, doesn't help you answer the hard questions about status.

When you're measuring the effectiveness of efforts to improve delivery performance, you tend to try to measure activity rather than outcomes. It seems only natural, because you're changing the way you work and you want to be sure team members are doing things the "new" way and not falling back on habit.

In reality, the simplest and most effective way to gauge the effect of new practices on delivery performance is to measure delivery performance directly. The effects of any new practices will be reflected in the outcomes the team achieves.

As Eliyahu Goldratt said in *The Haystack Syndrome*, "Tell me how you measure me, and I will tell you how I will behave" (North River Press, 1990). When you measure team members' use of specific practices, they will make sure the numbers can't come back to haunt them at performance reviews. Measuring the adoption of new practices is almost certain to cause undesired behaviors while providing no useful information about the effectiveness of the new practices. By measuring outcomes, you can see the effects of any changes you have made in process or practices in a way that points no finger of blame at anyone.

3.5   *Metric: Velocity*

Question(s) answered
- Is the team delivering production-ready solution increments in each time-boxed iteration?
- Is the team's delivery rate consistent and predictable?

Description
- Quantity of work completed per time-boxed iteration
- Value
- Reducing variation in velocity improves planning predictability
- Ensuring that production-ready solution increments are delivered in each iteration maximizes the business value delivered.

Dependencies
- Approach: any
- Process model: time-boxed
- Delivery mode: discrete project

Success factors
- *Proper* use of a time-boxed iterative process model, fixed-length iterations, *production-ready* solution increments delivered in *each iteration*.

3.5.1   *When to use velocity*

Velocity is typically used as the basis to forecast a team's likely delivery performance in the near future based on empirical observation of their performance in the recent past. It provides a predictable basis for short-term planning, because it's based on observations of the team's actual performance rather than on estimates, promises, or stretch goals.

Velocity can be a useful measure when used appropriately, but it's sensitive to a number of factors. The team must use a consistent method of sizing or estimating work items, such as story points or ideal hours; or they can count the number of completed work items. The team must use a time-boxed iterative process model in which they deliver production-ready solution increments in each iteration. Given those prerequisites, you can count the number of points or hours of work the team completes in each iteration to obtain the velocity for that iteration.

For planning purposes, a series of three or more consecutive observations of velocity gives you a reasonably accurate idea of how much work the team is likely to deliver in the next iteration, provided there are no radical changes in team composition or resource availability. Because it's based on empirical observation of reality, velocity isn't vulnerable to estimation error, external pressure to deliver an arbitrary scope, optimism, or wishful thinking. A common practice is to use a rolling window of three or four iterations' worth of velocity observations as the basis to forecast delivery performance in the next one or two iterations.

As a trailing indicator, consistent velocity over time indicates the team is planning and executing their work well. Extreme variations in velocity indicate possible problems in delivery. As a leading indicator, a series of velocity observations supports forecasting.

3.5.2   *An adaptive project*

Assume you're measuring team performance on an adaptive software development project using a time-boxed iterative process model. You and the team are interested in improving delivery performance, and you plan to continue using a time-boxed process model. (The latter point is important because velocity is dependent on the use of a time-boxed iterative process model. If you were considering changing this, then velocity would be a poor metric to monitor improvement.) You're tracking the team's velocity, and you see a pattern like that shown in figure 3.1.

Normally, a team will find its own normal velocity after three or four iterations of working together on the same project. Consistent velocity enables you to predict the team's future performance with a reasonable degree of confidence. When velocity is erratic, as in this example, it's difficult to use empirical observations of the delivery rate to predict future performance.

One implication is that the team may have to resort to time-based estimation of individual work items as the basis for short-term planning. This is less reliable than projecting future performance based on empirical observations of past performance. When short-term planning is unreliable, project stakeholders tend to lose confidence in the team's delivery commitments. There's often a domino effect on delivery performance, morale, quality, and trust.

Apart from predictability, there are implications for the team's general delivery effectiveness, as well. An implication of erratic velocity is that the team is leaving features unfinished in some or all iterations. According to the time-boxed iterative model, the team is expected to deliver production-ready solution increments at a fairly steady rate throughout the project, once they have settled into their normal velocity. The team receives no credit for partially completed work items in the iteration when work was started. Instead, they receive full credit in the iteration when the work is completed.

The pattern shown usually means the team is leaving some work items unfinished in iterations 1, 3, and 5 and completing them in iterations 2, 4, and 6, along with new

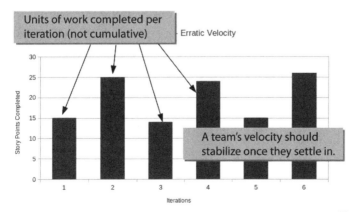

Figure 3.1   Erratic velocity

work. Neither the low nor the high velocity observations provide a dependable reading of the team's true delivery capacity.

In this case, velocity performs a diagnostic function. It highlights the fact that the team isn't delivering completed work items at a steady rate. Metrics can't tell you the exact reason for anomalies; they can only raise a flag. Potential causes of erratic velocity observations include the following:

- Work items are too large for the team to complete in the span of a single iteration. The team may need to learn how to decompose work items more effectively.

- Work items have dependencies on each other such that when one item is blocked, one or more additional items must be blocked as well. The team may need to learn how to define work items so that they're independent and can be executed in any sequence.

- Organizational structure makes a collaborative working style difficult to sustain. Typically this results from functional silos for development activities such as software testing and deployment, which tend to force teams into a waterfall sequence of hand-offs. The time-boxed iterative process model benefits from stable, cross-functional teams whose organization enables direct and continuous collaboration across roles. This makes it easier for teams to complete all the various activities necessary to deliver production-ready solution increments within the span of a single iteration.

- The team isn't applying the time-boxed iterative model rigorously. They may be allowing stakeholders to inject additional scope in the middle of the active iteration. According to the model, new scope is to be planned and prioritized in the product backlog (or equivalent artifact) and addressed in subsequent iterations. With this model, the iterations are, in effect, batches of work.

It's up to you to recognize erratic velocity as a signal of delivery problems and to perform appropriate root-cause analysis.

3.5.3 Anti-patterns

You've seen that velocity is susceptible to a variety of abuses when it's used to steer work in progress. It can also be abused when it's used to support process improvement.

SETTING TARGETS FOR VELOCITY IMPROVEMENT

Velocity works best as an empirical observation of a team's actual delivery performance. Velocity can support planning only when the reported numbers represent reality. Setting targets for velocity tends to drive undesired behaviors such as gaming the task estimates or user-story sizing to avoid punishment for failing to achieve management-dictated targets.

RELAXING THE DEFINITION OF "DONE"

It may be difficult to deliver truly complete, production-ready solution increments due to various organizational constraints. There's a temptation to make the velocity numbers appear more stable by softening the definition of *production-ready* so that it aligns with the team's current ability to complete work within the span of an iteration, rather than using the erratic velocity observations as a driver of process improvement. The point isn't to make things look good by adjusting the numbers; the point is to use real observations to identify opportunities for improvement.

COMPARING VELOCITY WHEN CHANGING THE PROCESS MODEL

Velocity is sensitive to the process model in use; it's meaningful only with a time-boxed iterative process. If your performance-improvement program includes a change from a time-boxed model to some other model, velocity can't provide a meaningful indication of whether the change has resulted in better or worse delivery performance. When your improvement program includes changing the process model, consider using process-agnostic metrics such as cycle time, throughput, and process-cycle efficiency for both the before and after measurements.

3.6   *Metric: Cycle time*

Question(s) answered
- What is the range of common-cause variation in the mean time to complete work items?
- How frequent are special-cause variations in mean completion time?
- What effect have process improvement efforts had on cycle time?

Description
- Mean time to complete a work item
- Value
- Reducing variation in cycle time improves planning predictability.
- Reducing variation in cycle time improves flow, which improves throughput and reduces waste.
- Reducing mean cycle time reduces time to market.
- Reducing mean cycle time increases throughput.
- Special-cause variation highlights opportunities for improvement in team practices.
- Common-cause variation highlights opportunities for systemic improvement.

Dependencies
- Approach: any
- Process model: any
- Delivery mode: any

Success factors
- Consistent definition of the start and end of each category of work item

In the last chapter, you saw how cycle time can be used to steer work in progress. You can also use cycle time to identify opportunities for performance improvement and to measure the effects of changes on delivery performance.

3.6.1   *When to use cycle time*

Use cycle time when you need to know the mean time it takes a team to complete a single work item, and when you want to know how much variation exists between the completion times for small and large work items. For purposes of process improvement, you're interested in reducing the mean cycle time as well as reducing the range of variation in completion times between the smallest and largest work items.

3.6.2   *Tracking improvement in predictability*

Assume that you're responsible for an adaptive software development project. The team delivers a production-ready solution increment on a regular release cadence. Stakeholders want to have a reasonable idea of how much work the team can complete in any given release.

You're using observations of mean cycle time to inform short-term planning, but the degree of variation in cycle time is large enough to have a negative impact on planning predictability. The team decides to address root causes for cycle-time variation. As a baseline, they use a recent series of cycle-time observations, shown in figure 3.2.

Discounting outliers, you see that variation attributable to common cause (systemic factors) ranges from 4.4 hours to 33.7 hours. Your planning is based on whole work items, not on estimated hours or story-point sizing. When a task might take anything from half a day to a week to complete, it's difficult to assure stakeholders of any particular delivery rate.

Planning is *accurate* in that most tasks will be completed in a time that falls within one standard deviation of the mean, but stakeholders would like it to be a bit more *precise* as well. If the team can take actions that reduce the variability of cycle time, they can provide better planning predictability.

Metrics can indicate potential areas of improvement, but they can't tell you the root causes of problems or suggest solutions. The team begins to look for causes of the variation in cycle time and makes changes in their work practices to try to reduce the variation.

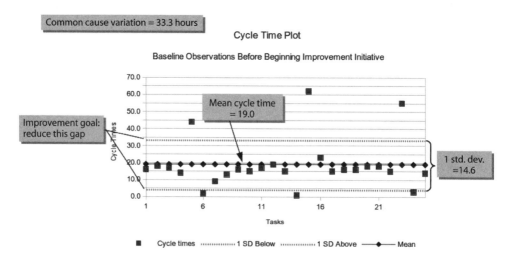

Figure 3.2   Baseline cycle-time observations

Many factors may contribute to cycle-time variation, and an exhaustive treatment of root-cause analysis is beyond the scope of this book. Some possibilities include the following:

- Work items aren't decomposed into similarly sized chunks.
- Work items tend to have non-obvious technical challenges that emerge only after development begins.
- The team has dependencies on external groups for needed resources or assets, such as test data, servers, or databases; and delays in obtaining these services are unpredictable.
- The system under development must interact with external systems that are unreliable or not always available.

Whatever the root causes in this case, let's assume that the team takes actions intended to reduce variability in cycle time. After a couple of release cycles, you see the change in cycle-time observations shown in figure 3.3.

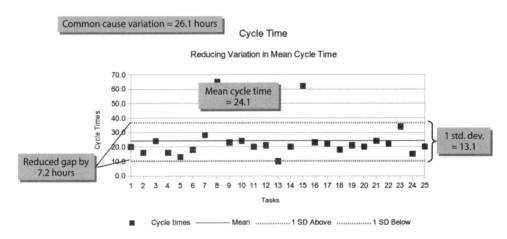

Figure 3.3 Cycle-time observations after changes in process or methods

The team has succeeded in reducing the variation in cycle time, but the mean cycle time has increased. That means the team has improved planning predictability but is taking more time to deliver than before.

3.6.3 Tracking improvement in flow

Let's say you and the team want to reduce mean cycle time so that you can complete more work items in each release cadence. In other words, you want to increase throughput, and to do that you intend to reduce cycle time. Assume that your starting point is the cycle-time plot in figure 3.3.

The team investigates possible root causes for long cycle times. The details are out of scope for this book, but here are a few typical causes for reference:

- The team takes on too many work items simultaneously (too much work in process [WIP]).
- Handoffs of interim artifacts between functional specialists cause delays as incomplete work waits for attention.
- Work items encounter blocks to wait for clarification of requirements or other information or services needed to continue.
- The team doesn't have adequate automation in place for testing, configuration, or deployment.
- Team members are physically dispersed, and formal meetings must be convened to carry out routine development activities such as requirements elaboration, design brainstorming, code reviews, and agreeing on architectural standards.
- Software engineering practices tend to create defects that must be discovered and corrected after the fact.
- The team has a low *bus number*, that is, only one or two individuals possess critical knowledge or skills, and they're a bottleneck in the process.
- Team members aren't trusted to make decisions, and the designated decision-makers are a bottleneck in the process.

Let's say the team analyzes possible root causes for long cycle times and makes adjustments in their process, collaboration, and technical practices. After a couple of release cycles, you observe the changes in cycle time shown in figure 3.4.

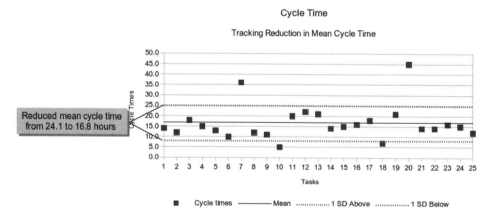

Figure 3.4   Mean cycle time reduced after changes in process or methods

In this example, the team succeeded in reducing mean cycle time from 24.1 to 16.8 hours, or from about three days to complete a typical work item to about two days.

3.6.4 *Tracking responsiveness to special-cause variation*

So far, we've ignored cycle times that vary from the mean by more than one standard deviation. The reason is that they represent a different category of issues.

We consider variation within one standard deviation of the mean to represent *common-cause* variation—that is, variation that results from the interoperation of the moving parts of the system (the organization). To change cycle-time variation in that range, you have to change the way work is generally organized, planned, and executed.

We consider variation beyond one standard deviation of the mean to represent *special-cause* variation—that is, variation caused by one-off, unexpected events. To deal with special-cause variation, you don't fundamentally change your organization, process, or technical practices. Instead, you take special action to respond to unusual events. Such action may include expediting a work item, *swarming* it (having team members temporarily stop other work and collaborate to complete the item), or temporarily waiving WIP limits to help the item flow through the process. As the team improves its flexibility to switch gears and deal with these issues, the improvement shows up in the cycle-time chart as smaller special-cause variation (see figure 3.5).

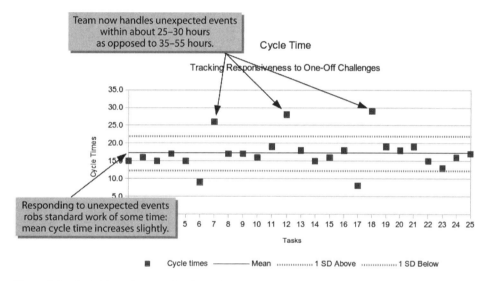

Figure 3.5 Cycle-time changes after improving responsiveness to special-cause variation

3.7   *Metric: Burn chart*

Question(s) answered
- Is the team moving work items through the process smoothly?

Description
- Indicates whether the team is piling up incomplete work and then scrambling to complete it at the end of a development cadence or iteration

Value
- Can help identify appropriate WIP limits to promote continuous flow

Dependencies
- Approach: any
- Process model: any
- Delivery mode: discrete project

Success factors

- Consistent understanding of what constitutes a work item (by whatever name)
- Explicit, demonstrable, binary definition of what it means to declare a work item complete

3.7.1 *When to use burn charts*

A burn chart shows the amount of work done (*burn-up chart*) or the amount of work remaining to be done (*burn-down chart*). You've seen how this can be used to help steer WIP toward a defined goal. A burn chart can also point to irregularities in flow.

Use a burn chart to visualize how smoothly the team completes work. When the team achieves continuous flow, the burn chart will rise toward the target (burn-up format) or descend toward zero (burn-down format) fairly smoothly, with few stalls or bumps along the way. A burn chart reveals interference with continuous flow when the line remains flat or erratically rises and falls.

3.7.2 *Adaptive development project using a time-boxed iterative process model*

Assume that you're monitoring delivery improvement efforts on an adaptive development project. The team is using a time-boxed iterative process model with a two-week iteration length. You and the team have noticed that many work items remain in flight throughout most of each iteration. Toward the end of an iteration, the team is under pressure to complete many outstanding work items.

Let's also assume that the methodology in use calls for user stories as the requirements artifacts. The user stories aren't estimated in terms of time but are sized relative to one another based on a unitless scheme such as story points, units, or T-shirt sizes. We'll use the term *story points* here.

As you know, a burn-down chart and a burn-up chart show the same information. There's no need to show examples of both. We'll use the burn-down format here. A burn-down chart showing progress in a typical iteration for your team (let's call it iteration 9) looks like figure 3.6.

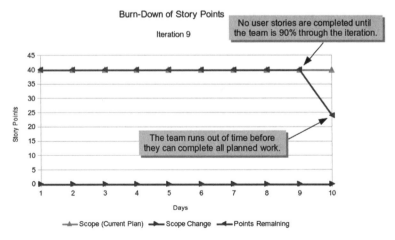

Figure 3.6   Iteration burn-down: baseline for improvement

The recurring pattern is causing stress, software defects, and incomplete work items. The stress leads to lower morale, lack of focus, and careless work; the defects create failure demand for non-value-add work for correction; the incomplete work items carry over into subsequent iterations, reducing the team's delivery capacity by pushing out planned work and by increasing the amount of context-switching overhead between planned work and unplanned defect correction; and the apparent inability of the team to deliver on a predictable schedule reduces stakeholder trust, which leads to increased oversight and administrative overhead, in turn feeding the cycle of slower delivery.

As always, the metrics don't tell you the root causes. Some possible causes of this pattern include the following:

- User stories have dependencies on one another.
- User stories represent horizontal decomposition of technical tasks rather than vertical slices of features.
- The team has too much WIP.
- Testing is deferred until late in the iteration.
- The team has a dependency on external resources to provide test data or test environments and doesn't control the availability of those resources.
- The team has a low bus number; one or two individuals are in demand to support specific aspects of many stories, creating a bottleneck.
- The team doesn't recognize the value of continuous flow and regards the iteration as a whole as a single batch of work. The attitude is that delivering everything at once at the end of the iteration is just as good as delivering each user story as soon as it's complete.

Whatever the causes, assume that the team addresses some of the problems and shows improvement in smoothing their work flow by iteration 12 (see figure 3.7).

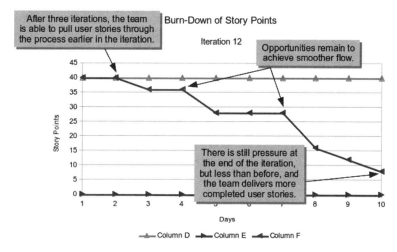

Figure 3.7 Iteration burn-down after first round of improvement

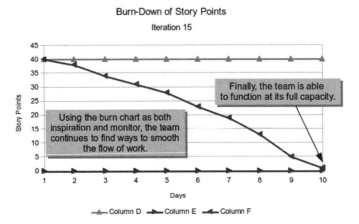

Figure 3.8   Iteration burn-down after second round of improvement

The team continues to identify and address the root causes of erratic delivery within each iteration. They improve their work flow still further by iteration 15, as shown in figure 3.8.

Notice that this example spans six iterations. If the team is running two-week iterations, which is a typical iteration length for teams using this sort of process, that means the improvements required 12 weeks to bear fruit. Even when people routinely and mindfully improve their work throughout each day, you can't expect dramatic improvements to occur quickly.

3.8   *Metric: Cumulative flow*

Question(s) answered
- Where is the bottleneck (also known as the *constraint*, per Theory of Constraints) in the process?
- Which segments of the process account for the greatest proportion of total lead time?
- Where does incomplete work pile up due to high WIP?
- Where is flow irregular due to low WIP?

Description
- Provides a visual indication of how smoothly the work flows through the process

Value
- Can point to segments of the process that are affected by resource availability
- Can indicate "bus number" problems where work waits for scarce skills
- Can help identify appropriate WIP limits to promote continuous flow

Dependencies
- Approach: any
- Process model: any
- Delivery mode: any

Success factors
- Consistent understanding of what constitutes a work item (by whatever name)
- Explicit, demonstrable, binary definition of what it means to declare a work item complete

3.8.1   When to use a cumulative flow diagram

You've seen how a cumulative flow diagram (CFD) can help to steer work in progress. A CFD is also useful for tracking the effects of process-improvement efforts.

A CFD provides a visualization of several interesting factors at a glance. These include throughput, lead time, cycle time, queue depth, and work remaining. When one region of the CFD grows wider, it indicates a logjam or bottleneck in the process.

3.8.2   An adaptive project

Let's assume that the team is interested in improving continuous flow. The starting point is the situation shown by the CFD presented in chapter 2; see figure 3.9.

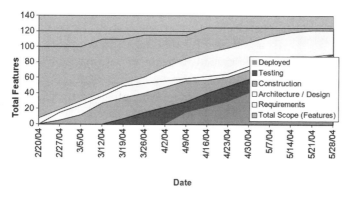

Figure 3.9   Cumulative flow diagram

Here you assume that each work item progresses through a series of states on its journey from concept to cash. With some processes, the states correspond to discrete steps in a linear model. In that case, the transitions between states could represent hand-offs of interim artifacts between functional specialists. With other processes, the states don't suggest hand-offs or functional silos. Instead, they represent stages in the evolution of features as they're realized in code. The CFD works equally well with either sort of process by making visible certain key information about flow.

Let's assume that this project takes work items through the following states, via whatever process model and working style the team may be using:

- Requirements
- Architecture / Design
- Construction
- Testing
- Deployed

Figure 3.10 shows the annotated version of the CFD from the chapter 2.

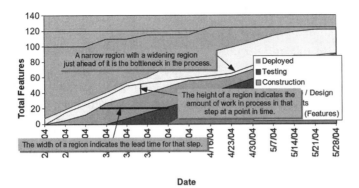

Figure 3.10 Cumulative flow diagram, annotated

The CFD is telling you that incomplete work is piling up just ahead of the Architecture / Design state. At a glance, you can see that Architecture / Design is the *constraint* (Theory of Constraints term) or *bottleneck* (general term) in the process. Once you've identified the constraint in a process, you can begin to improve flow by adjusting the WIP limit on the state immediately ahead of the constraint.

Are we getting ahead of ourselves? I've been saying all along that metrics can't tell you what the underlying problems are—they can only raise a flag to get your attention. Yet in this case, after glancing at a CFD for three seconds, we've concluded that the team needs to adjust WIP limits.

You can be confident that adjusting WIP limits is a good first step because you know that the maximum throughput of any process is dictated by the capacity of its constraint. You haven't identified the factors that cause Architecture / Design to be the constraint in this case. You're slowing the accumulation of incomplete work, or *inventory* (a form of waste per the Lean school of thought)—in this case, in the form of old requirements artifacts awaiting attention.

The five focusing steps

To be a bit more formal about it, you're applying the process-improvement mechanism defined by the Theory of Constraints (ToC). Like many process-improvement frameworks, ToC defines a plan-do-check-act (PDCA) cycle. It's called the five focusing steps. The steps are as follows:

1 Identify the constraint.

2 Exploit the constraint.

3 Subordinate the process to the constraint.

4 Elevate the capacity of the constraint.

5 Repeat.

The idea is that any process comprising more than a single step has a constraint—the step with the lowest capacity—and that you can maximize throughput by controlling where the constraint is located in the process and how its capacity is managed.

> The CFD helps you identify the constraint. That's step 1. Next, you ensure that the constrained step has all the resources and support necessary for it to function at its maximum capacity. Any delay in the constraint is a delay in the end-to-end process. Delays in other steps can be absorbed by managing queues between steps, but the constraint sets the pace of the entire process. This is what is meant by *exploiting* the constraint in step 2.
>
> Step 3 is to prevent the other steps in the process from operating faster than the constraint. To do so only creates WIP inventory, which is waste. This is what you're doing when you limit the WIP feeding into Architecture / Design by throttling Requirements. The CFD shows you where you need to do this in a visual way: the constraint appears as a narrow band with a wide band just ahead of it.
>
> For step 4—improving the capacity of the constraint—you have to perform root-cause analysis and make changes in your process, resource allocation, personnel, and/or technical practices. The CFD doesn't automatically tell you what to do in those areas.

Let's say the team determines that the reason Architecture / Design is the constraint is that only one team member is engaged in that activity, whereas two business analysts are busy creating requirements artifacts for the architect to consume. Not only can they produce interim artifacts faster than the architect can produce designs, but the architect also has to change the existing design to accommodate new requirements.

The team decides to take several actions to address the issue:

1   Limit the WIP in Requirements to match the capacity of the architect. This means the business analysts are sometimes idle; in the larger scheme of things, you don't want them to produce requirements artifacts too early and overload the architect, only to have the requirements change later. That would cause *rework*, another form of waste per the Lean school of thought. On the bright side, the analysts can now spend more time working with stakeholders to ensure that the requirements are of high quality and more time working with testers to ensure that test plans and test scripts are well aligned with requirements.

2   Exploit the constraint. Proactively remove any organizational barriers that might slow down the architect. Do everything possible to keep the constraint operating at its maximum capacity.

3   Elevate the constraint. Provide training and mentoring of other technical team members so that they can begin to take on some of the Architecture / Design work. If they need additional software tools or server resources to enable them to work more effectively, provide those items. If they need to be relieved from attending meetings that aren't related to the project, substitute others in those meetings.

4   Repeat—see where the constraint has moved.

As a result of the team's improvement efforts, you see changes in the CFD, as shown in figure 3.11.

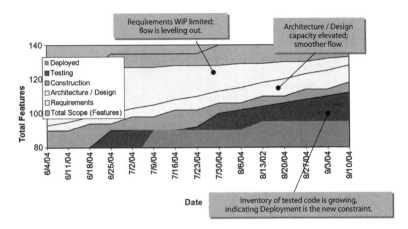

Figure 3.11   Cumulative flow diagram after process changes

Over time, the impact of the team's improvements becomes evident in the CFD. By limiting WIP in the Requirements state, the team was able to use (or discard) the accumulated inventory of requirements artifacts while enabling the business analysts to spend more time collaborating with stakeholders. By increasing the capacity of the Architecture / Design state, they moved the constraint elsewhere in the process. The new constraint is showing up in Deployment. The widening band of Testing indicates that tested code is piling up, ready to be deployed.

   This shows the team where to begin when they repeat the five focusing steps. Deployable code that isn't deployed represents unrealized business value. The team can now focus on improving the deployment process, using CFD as a practical guide.

3.9   *Metric: Process cycle efficiency*

Question(s) answered
- Where is time being lost to non-value-add activity?

Description
- Shows the proportion of value-add time to total lead time

Value
- Highlights the time sinks in the process
- Can help identify appropriate WIP limits to promote continuous flow

Dependencies
- Approach: any
- Process model: any
- Delivery mode: any

Success factors
- Track value-add time and non-value-add time explicitly
- Pay attention to non-value-add time when work is in an active state, caused by waits and context-switching overhead

3.9.1   When to use process cycle efficiency

Use process cycle efficiency (PCE) when you want to understand the proportion of total lead time in which value is added to the product. The higher the PCE, the greater the proportion of available time that's being used in value-add activity.

PCE is a powerful metric that can provide profound insight into how time is used in a process. Despite its usefulness, PCE isn't often tracked. This may be due to the difficulty of collecting the raw data.

Consider the software development process outlined in figure 3.12. This assumes the up-front work for determining the business capabilities to be realized, risk management, market research, funding, and other big-picture issues have been completed. You're looking at the world from the perspective of a single software development team. The team has received the list of software features they're charged with developing. Obviously, this is only one piece of the puzzle, but remember the scope of this book is tracking progress and monitoring process improvement at the team level, not the enterprise level. Bear in mind that many processes are possible, and the steps shown in the example may not correspond with the steps in your real-world process.

This is a crude version of a *value stream map* (VSM). The tool comes from Lean manufacturing, a domain where it's used to understand how time is spent in a process. The *value stream* is the series of steps from the beginning of a process until the final product is delivered. The simplified version of the VSM as adapted to software development work only shows *queues* or *buffers*, where work is waiting to be addressed, and *active* states, where people are bringing work items closer to completion. The queues are depicted as triangles with the point downward, and the active states are depicted as rectangles.

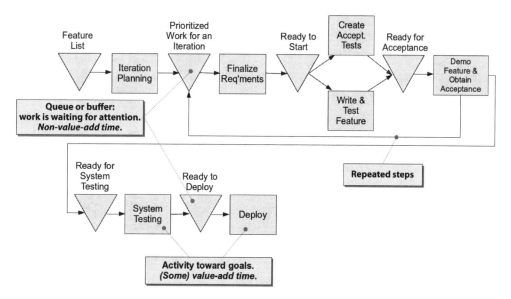

Figure 3.12   Value stream map

As work progresses, it moves between queues and active states. When it's in a queue, the work is waiting for attention. By definition, no value is being added to a work item that's in a queue. All the time a work item spends in queues is *non-value-add* (NVA) time. Any time spent actively working on an item is considered *value-add* (VA) time. The metric *process cycle efficiency* (PCE) is the proportion of VA time to total lead time.

3.9.2   *Non-value-add time in queues*

It's easy enough to count the NVA time of work items in queues. It's the total time the work items spend in the queue.

For example, in the CFD example from chapter 2, a quantity of requirements artifacts were piling up ahead of the Architecture / Design state. All the time those artifacts were waiting for attention was part of the total *lead time* to deliver the features they described, and all that time was NVA time. The analysts may have felt as if they were doing well to get ahead of the requirements elaboration work, but in reality they were only creating unfinished goods inventory and reducing PCE.

Let's assume the VSM shown in figure 3.12 represents the work flow in your project. You can start to collect raw data toward PCE by tracking the *mean* time a work item spends in each queue and in each action state. Let's plug some numbers into the VSM to see how that might look (see figure 3.13).

This gives you an average lead time per feature of 242.6 days, of which an item spends an average of 47.6 days in an active state. If you assume all the time spent in an active state is VA time, that gives you a PCE of about 20%. That means you're adding value to the product about 20% of the time that you're working. When you consider the various impacts on your time, such as meetings, supporting regulatory requirements, and unavoidable administrative tasks, that doesn't seem so bad.

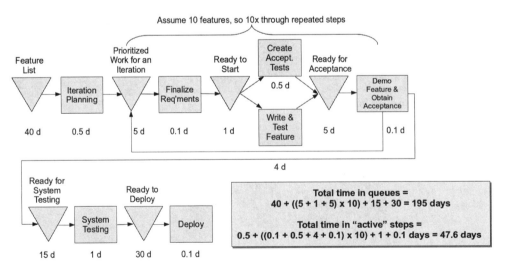

Figure 3.13   Value stream map with time data

3.9.3   *Non-value-add time in active states*

Before you celebrate, however, you need to remember that you aren't adding value to work items every moment they're designated in an active state. PCE starts to give you useful information to support process-improvement efforts when you consider how the time is spent when you believe an item is in progress.

Let's consider the activity labeled Write & Test Feature. According to your VSM, this activity occurs once per feature in the course of an iteration, and it takes an average of four days. When you take a closer look at what happens when programmers are writing code, you might see that they're multitasking across multiple work items simultaneously. After all, an iteration isn't 242.6 days long. It's only 10 days long.

Multitasking, or *context switching*, takes a toll on a person's effectiveness. When performing creatively intensive work such as writing software, a person enters a state colloquially known as *the zone*. (This is what psychologist Mihaly Czikszentmihalyi called *flow*, although that's a very different meaning than *flow* in Lean thinking.) While in the zone (or in a state of flow), the programmer is effective at producing correct code quickly. When the person switches contexts, they drop out of the zone. It takes 10–20 minutes to get back into the zone again.

Context switching occurs for a variety of reasons. If someone approaches the programmer's desk and asks a question, it breaks flow. If programmers are called into formal meetings periodically throughout the day, it breaks flow. If programmers try to juggle too many work items simultaneously, they can't maintain flow for long. The end result? Delay, defects, and rework.

Let's plug some numbers into the VSM to see how this might look (see figure 3.14). When you take into account all the time lost during active states, when work items are marked "in progress," you can see the relative amount of time you're adding value to the product. This gives you a basis to look for ways to increase the proportion of VA time to total lead time.

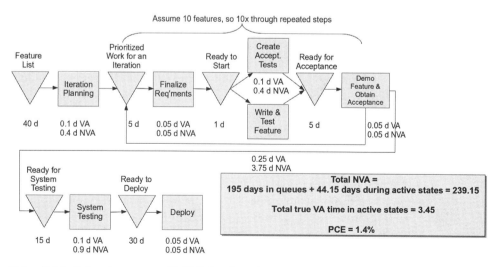

Figure 3.14   Value stream map with NVA time in active states

In this example, you see that it takes the team an average of 242.6 days to bring a feature from concept to production, and that you spend about 1.4% of that time directly adding value to the feature you're developing.

3.9.4 *What is normal PCE?*

The figure 1.4% might seem a bit low at first glance, if you haven't calculated PCE before. In my consulting work, I usually see PCE in the range of 1–2% in software development organizations. It often comes as a shock to people. Many assume their process is around 70–80% efficient.

It turns out this is an unrealistic expectation. I've read that world-class manufacturing operations can achieve PCE of 25% or a bit more, whereas world-class product-development processes top out at around 5%. This difference is due to the inherent unpredictability of product-development work compared with manufacturing operations.

It might not sound like much, but improving PCE from 1.5% to 3% can have a profound and visible effect on delivery. It isn't as difficult to achieve as you may expect, because it often involves discontinuing or minimizing NVA activities rather than learning wholly new ways to perform VA activities.

3.9.5 *Moving the needle*

Your PCE may suggest to you that root-cause analysis is in order and that you might consider changes to improve performance. PCE doesn't directly tell you what to change. Although this book isn't about root-cause analysis, I will suggest a few typical issues that lead to low PCE in many software development organizations:

- *A focus on resource utilization instead of throughput.* This mentality causes people to feel as if something is wrong when they aren't busy. They try to stay busy no matter what. Consider the case when you have several work items on your plate. Item 1 is of high priority to the business, and the rest are of relatively lower priority. You work on Item 1 until you hit a block, and you send a request for information to someone in the organization who can help you. Meanwhile, to stay productive, you start working on Item 2. You receive the answer you need to resume Item 1, but now you're busy with Item 2 and it isn't convenient to stop cold. You continue with Item 2 until you hit a block. Just then, a colleague asks for your help with an unrelated issue. You help them and then finally return to Item 1. You've succeeded in maximizing your own *utilization*, but you've reduced *throughput* by robbing time from Item 1. It would have been better for the organization had you been available to resume Item 1 the moment you received the answer to your question, because Item 1 had a higher priority than anything else on your to-do list. You're more effective by being available for high-priority work than by being arbitrarily busy with low-priority work.
- *Juggling too many tasks at once.* In Lean terms, this is called *high WIP*. High WIP causes context-switching overhead, which reduces effectiveness. There's an

assumption in some organizations that the best way to complete many work items is to start them all at once. Some managers like this because it appears as if all the work items are in progress—the project-management tool shows them in an active state. In reality, you can finish a long list of tasks in less time by tackling them one or two at a time than you can by starting them all and then trying to context-switch between them.

- *Too much up-front analysis and design.* With traditional methods of software development, the assumption was that you had to work out all the details of solution design before beginning the programming work. What we've learned over the years is that requirements go stale as stakeholders and teams learn more and more about the evolving solution in the course of a project. The stale requirements have to be revisited and modified and in some cases discarded. All the work that went into them initially turns out to be wasted effort. The huge pile of stale requirements shows up in the PCE calculation as unfinished work waiting in a queue.

- *A rigid series of hand-offs between functional specialists.* This sort of work flow causes unfinished inventory to accumulate between active states, waiting for the appropriate functional specialist to become available to pick it up.

- *Buffer-management problems.* In a continuous-flow process, the queues or buffers are designed to keep the work flowing smoothly even when different steps in the process are operating at different speeds. Because product-development work is inherently unpredictable, there will be times when programming moves faster than requirements elaboration, or when testing moves faster than programming, and so forth. When a downstream step is moving faster than the step that feeds it, you need some work in the buffer for the downstream step to pick up so the process doesn't grind to a halt. On the other hand, when there's too much work in a buffer, it starts to go stale. Finding the right queue depth is part of managing a continuous-flow process.

Use with caution

PCE can provide powerful insight into the amount of lead time that goes to waste. Most people in the IT field are unaccustomed to thinking about time this way, and they accept a lot of process waste as normal and even inevitable. It's useful to show the real numbers from time to time, if only to maintain awareness of the importance of throughput versus utilization.

But the difficulty of collecting accurate raw data for PCE makes it impractical for regular use. Although some electronic tools can sum the time in queues separately from the time in active states, no tools exist that can distinguish between VA and NVA time within an active state. That's where you can find surprising and assumption-busting information for process improvement.

(continued)

I use PCE to obtain supporting data when I have other reasons to believe there are issues caused by people's assumptions about utilization and throughput, and in particular about the advisability of high WIP levels. To collect the raw data, I ask individual team members to make note of each instance when they switch contexts. This is burdensome and easy to forget, so I want people to go to the extra trouble only temporarily and only to meet a specific improvement need.

You can get a coarse-grained sense of the proportion of NVA time to lead time by tracking cycle time and paying attention to spans of time when work items are in NVA states. PCE can expose a deeper layer of truth about wasted time, but only at the cost of manual data collection.

3.10   *Metric: Version control history*

Question(s) answered
- Which files are modified most frequently?
- Which files have been checked out to make corrections or fixes on a recurring basis?

Description
- The history of commits made to the version control system
- Value
- Points to areas of the code base that are frequently changed
- Helps you identify where to focus your efforts to achieve the highest payback

Dependencies
- Approach: any
- Process model: any
- Delivery mode: any

Success factors
- A version control system is in use.
- Team members are diligent about providing comments when they commit changes.

3.10.1   *When to use version control history*

Use version control history to see which source code files and configuration files are most frequently checked out and modified. This points the team to the files that are most worthy of their attention for refactoring to reduce technical debt. Files that rarely change may not be worth the effort.

Version control history falls into the category of technical metrics. Version control systems retain a historical record of all the checkouts and commits that have occurred. In most cases, the Pareto Principle or 80/20 rule applies to code units—most of the changes to an existing code base occur in a subset of modules.

It takes little effort to collect the data. Version control systems will output the commit history on request. If you sort the list in descending order by frequency, you'll see the modules that tend to receive the most changes. By correlating that list with static code-analysis metrics (described shortly), you can identify the modules that may benefit the most from refactoring.

You can examine the commit comments from the version control system, as well. Look for indications of which commits pertained to bug fixes and which to feature enhancements.

If many bug fixes appear to touch the same modules, those modules may benefit from a closer examination. You may discover that one or more modules are badly designed or messy, and it's difficult for the team to modify them without creating regressions.

You may also be able to match frequently committed modules with categories of bugs. This may lead you to discover that certain *concerns* or *aspects* (logging, security, exception handling, and so on) of the product aren't well designed or well factored. This can lead the team to an architectural refactoring exercise.

If one or a few modules seem to be involved in nearly all feature enhancements, it may or may not be a red flag. There is a *code smell* known as *god class* that afflicts many object-oriented code bases. A god class knows too much and must be involved in too many different things to satisfy general object-oriented design principles.

A module that isn't frequently checked out and modified may not be worth investigating even if static code-analysis metrics point to structural problems in the code. The adage "If it ain't broke, don't fix it" applies.

3.11 Metric: Static code-analysis metrics

Question(s) answered
- Does the code have structural problems?

Description
- Software build systems usually include features to analyze the source code statically (without executing the code) to look for well-known structural problems.

Value
- Helps you focus technical debt reduction efforts in areas that are likely to yield payback

Dependencies
- Approach: any
- Process model: any
- Delivery mode: any

Success factors
- Static code-analysis features are installed and enabled in the automated build for the project.

3.11.1 When to use static code-analysis metrics

Certain kinds of issues with source code can be detected by analyzing the source code without compiling or executing the application. Static code-analysis tools perform this sort of analysis. You can use static code analysis to identify the source code files that have the most serious structural problems. This helps the team understand which files are worthy of their attention for refactoring to reduce technical debt. Static code-analysis metrics are often used in conjunction with version-control history to zero in on the files that are the most valuable targets for a refactoring effort.

Static code-analysis metrics are technical metrics. It's possible to detect problems or potential problems in software by analyzing the source code alone, without building the product or running tests against it. A wide range of algorithms have been developed to do this, and an exhaustive review of them is beyond the scope of this book. You should know that the development tools your team is using can probably provide a wealth of information about the quality of the code automatically. Based on that feedback, the team can take action to improve code quality.

The reason to care about code quality is that complicated and messy code is hard to modify safely. This makes every feature enhancement take more time and cost more money than necessary. The accumulation of technical problems over time is called *technical debt* or *design debt*, and it's a leading cause of slowdowns in development and of premature death of production systems.

Static code-analysis tools generally focus on seven key areas, sometimes known as the *seven axes of code quality* or the *seven deadly sins of programmers*:

- *Complexity*—Static code-analysis tools look for a couple of types of complexity. The first is *cyclomatic complexity*, which checks the depth of nested conditional statements in code. A high value for cyclomatic complexity may mean that the code is difficult to understand and, therefore, difficult to modify safely. In some cases, it may only mean the section of code in question is inherently complicated.

  The second type of complexity is known as *response for class* (RFC), and it mainly applies to object-oriented programming languages. The algorithm is based on counting the total number of method calls and the number of unique method calls in a class.

  Excessive complexity of either type can make the code hard to understand as well as time-consuming and risky to change.

- *Duplication*—Sometimes there are snippets of identical code in multiple places in the code base. There can also be less-obvious forms of duplication, such as functions or methods that perform almost the same processing and that differ only in superficial ways, or utilities in different third-party packages that perform the same functions, or classes in different packages that have similar or overlapping responsibilities.

- *Test coverage*—Unit tests are the most fine-grained set of automated tests applied to a code base. They're usually written in the same programming language as the production code and stored in the same project as the production code in the version-control system. For those reasons, static code-analysis tools can easily check code coverage at the unit level. The appropriate coverage depends on the level of validation built into the programming language itself and the amount of code that can be generated automatically by development tools. One hundred percent test coverage isn't usually necessary or desirable, but in general higher coverage is better than lower coverage.

- *Coding standards*—A code base that generally follows the same conventions for names and structure will tend to be less error-prone and easier to maintain than a code base that exhibits a hodgepodge of different conventions and styles. Code-analysis tools can be configured to block a commit when the code to be checked in doesn't follow a set of defined standards. Alternatively, tools can be configured to notify you when code violates standards without preventing the build from proceeding.

- *Comments*—Code that includes excessive source comments can be confusing to follow, both because of the general clutter created by the comments and because comments tend to quickly get out of sync with the code they describe. On the other hand, there are occasions when explanatory comments help people understand the intent of the code or warn about potential side effects when the code is modified. Static code-analysis tools can apply heuristics to warn you when it seems as if there are too many or too few comments in the source code. Source lines that are commented out and left in place are also questionable.

- *Potential bugs*—Some static code-analysis tools look for structural patterns in the code that can lead to predictable problems with respect to maintainability, security, testability, efficiency, reliability, portability, and similar factors. These can provide useful early warnings of potential problems.

- *Architectural issues*—Structural patterns in the code can point to architectural issues. In large, complicated applications that comprise multiple separately deployable components, circular or cyclic dependencies between components can lead to serious problems in building and deploying the application. This means a module in component A has a dependency on a module in component B, and a different module in component B has a dependency on some other module in component A. A programmer working on a small subset of the code base may well overlook this sort of problem, and static code-analysis tools can bring it to your attention.

Some tools can validate the structure of the code base against a set of architectural constraints the team defines. This can guard against inappropriate access across different architectural tiers or layers in the application.

Dependencies between application components and third-party libraries, and between one application component and another, can be detected and reported by static code-analysis tools. This information can help teams identify potential opportunities for improvement of code quality as well as exposure to reported bugs in libraries.

A general guideline for good software design is to strive for *high cohesion* and *loose coupling*. The two generally vary inversely with respect to one another. *Cohesion* is a property of code whereby things that have to change together are kept together in the source. *Coupling* refers to the degree to which different modules depend on each other, or must know about each other. The rule of thumb about high cohesion and low coupling applies to any source code and isn't specific to any programming paradigm. Static code-analysis tools can look for structural patterns that suggest high coupling.

3.12   *Metric: Niko Niko calendar*

Question(s) answered

- How does the team's emotional state change over time?

Description

- Based on a simple check-in once per day by each team member, the calendar tracks mood using just three states: positive, neutral, and negative. There's no in-depth psychological analysis.

Value

- Raises a warning about possible systemic issues that are affecting team morale
- Can sometimes provide earlier warning of delivery issues than process-oriented or technical metrics, because low morale usually leads to other problems

Dependencies

- Approach: any
- Process model: any
- Delivery mode: any

Success factors

- The team must voluntarily agree to participate in providing the data.

3.12.1   *When to use the Niko Niko calendar*

Use a Niko Niko calendar (http://www.nikoniko.co/) when you want to get a general sense of the team's morale, especially when you want to see how their morale changes over time. When team members always report that they feel positive, it may indicate managerial or political drivers causing them to believe they must pretend to be happy or satisfied all the time. When they always report that they feel negative, it may indicate factors in the work environment that are causing frustration, such as insufficient technical resources, excessive overtime requirements, or difficulties coordinating work with other teams. When team members always report feeling neutral, it may indicate the team is disengaged, perhaps due to monotony or boredom or perhaps because they're burned out from past frustration. When the calendar reflects a normal flow of common emotional states, it doesn't indicate any problems with morale.

3.12.2   *Examples*

Figure 3.15 shows one of the early examples of a Niko Niko calendar that appeared online several years ago. The title reads "August's Niko-Niko Calendar," and the photo shows the latter part of the month. Days of the month are listed across, and team members are listed down (their names have been covered).

Each day at the same time, each team member places a smiley face next to their name. Exactly three kinds of smileys are used: a blue one denotes a negative state of

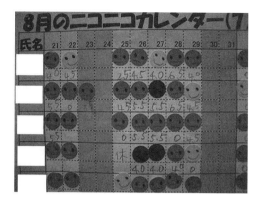

Figure 3.15   Niko Niko calendar

mind, red denotes neutral, and yellow denotes positive. Team members give no expla-
nation for the smileys they choose, and there's no questioning. (The numbers below
the smileys are unrelated.)

The example indicates team members usually feel neutral about their work, sometimes they're positive about it, and occasionally they're negative about it. The Niko
Niko calendar provides insight into the team's morale without being intrusive.

In Western countries, people have taken the liberty of changing the color-coding
scheme to one that aligns with Western conventions. They use green for positive, yellow for neutral, and red for negative, as in the example in figure 3.16, from Germany
(thanks to Berndt Schiffer).

SEPTEMBER 2011	1	2	3	4	5	6	7
BERND	🙂	😐	▨	▨	😐	🙂	☹
MARIKO	🙂	🙂	▨	▨	☹	🙂	🙂
ALEX	🙂	😐	▨	▨	🙂	😐	☹
MEIKE	☹	🙂	▨	▨	🙂	🙂	☹
STEFAN	🙂	🙂	▨	▨	😐	😐	🙂

**Figure 3.16   Niko Niko calendar
from Germany**

The color scheme isn't important. The key points are as follows:

- There are exactly three states.
- There's no attempt to depict any sort of precision about exactly how positive or
  negative a person feels.
- There's no connection with any real or perceived causes for feeling any particular way.
- There's no discussion or interrogation of team members regarding their
  choices.

You're interested in seeing patterns and trends in the team's mood over time, not in investigating specific cases.

The Niko Niko calendar provides interesting information when used in conjunction with other metrics. You can get a good sense of where to begin your root-cause analysis when you see overlapping patterns across process metrics, technical metrics, and human metrics. We'll explore some of these patterns in chapter 4. For now, here are some patterns to look for in the Niko Niko calendar alone.

3.12.3 *Happy Camper*

Let's say you're using the Niko Niko calendar with your team, and you see a pattern like that shown in figure 3.17. Most team members are in a neutral mood most days and are sometimes positive or negative. But look at Simon. He seems to be happy all the time. Does this seem reasonable? Simon is on your team, so you know him better than I. But when I see a pattern like this, it makes me wonder what's going on.

Figure 3.17   Niko Niko Happy Camper pattern

Does Simon fear reprisals if he publicly indicates he's less than ecstatic about the project? If so, there could be a problem with management communication to the team. Is he genuinely a happy person who tends to look on the bright side of things? If so, then there's no problem. Is he gaming the system in such a way that he off-loads his tasks to others and plays with new programming languages on company time? If so, it's a different problem. In any case, continuous positivity is so unusual in the workplace that it raises questions.

3.12.4 *Omega Wolf*

What if you see a pattern like that shown in figure 3.18? This is the opposite of the Happy Camper pattern. In this case, Kim is perpetually negative. It seems to make no difference what's going on with the project or how her teammates feel. I call this the Omega Wolf pattern.

Every wolf pack has the same social structure. There are four roles: Alpha (the leader of the pack), Beta (the likely successor to the Alpha), Subordinate (a standard pack member), and Omega. The Omega bears the brunt of the others' aggression and frustration and functions as a kind of emotional relief valve and social glue for the pack. Humans usually perceive this role as the lowest-ranking member of the pack,

Figure 3.18   Niko Niko Omega Wolf pattern

although that interpretation may amount to anthropomorphizing. Something in the nature of wolf life seems to require an Omega role in every pack.

In human organizations, social or political forces may be at play that create the need for a kind of Omega role. Traditional management science would hold that the negative person is the cause of the team's problems and would respond by firing that person. It's more likely that no one would have any positive days if not for the Omega team member. People generally don't want to be negative all the time; Kim is almost certainly providing a relief valve for the team's frustrations. Things would be worse without her.

Contemporary understanding holds that systemic factors constrain people's behavior, and when this behavioral pattern emerges, it signals some sort of organizational dysfunction. Firing the individual would only result in another team member assuming the Omega role, because organizational dynamics are creating the need for that role.

The only way to fix the problem is to identify and address the underlying organizational issues. In your position, you care about this because the team can't perform at its full capacity as long as the dysfunction continues to drive negative thinking.

3.12.5 Zombie Team

Assume that your team exhibits the pattern shown in figure 3.19. Here you see that every team member feels neutral about being at work every day. No matter how the project is going, no matter what holidays are coming up, no matter what good news or bad news they receive, they never feel either positive or negative. I call this the Zombie Team pattern. It means the team is disengaged.

Figure 3.19   Niko Niko Zombie Team pattern

There may be different causes for teams to slip into this frame of mind. If external management or stakeholders are micromanaging the team's work and dictating technical implementation decisions, then team members will disengage and cede ownership of the solution to the manger or stakeholder who wants to control details.

Another cause of zombie teams is the overzealous team coach. Hired by management from outside the organization to help improve the development and delivery process and/or technical practices, the coach wants to implement a predefined process or methodology, or wants the team to adopt specific technical practices. Often with the best intentions, this sort of coach takes ownership of the team's work practices, and the team members disengage.

Strangely enough, too much success can lead to zombie teams, as well. There are ongoing movements in the software industry to institute one or another process model or set of technical practices. The emphasis is on helping new teams get started with the new process and practices. Once a team has gotten started, there's relatively little support to help them sustain interest, enthusiasm, and discipline with the new practices. Teams can fall into a rut, repeating the new practices they have learned but losing the spark that got them started in the first place.

3.13 Metric: Emotional seismogram

Question(s) answered
- How did team members feel about how things were going in the course of the last iteration?

Description
- A technique used in heartbeat retrospectives to get a sense of the emotional shape of the iteration that just passed

Value
- Can help highlight issues that lead to emotional ups and downs of the team

Dependencies
- Approach: any
- Process model: any
- Delivery mode: any

Success factors
- Best when the team practices heartbeat retrospectives

3.13.1 When to use the emotional seismogram

This is an alternative to the Niko Niko calendar as a way to gauge the emotional state of team members. There are two ways to use it. First, you can ask team members to mark a point each day that represents how they feel about the work as of that moment. Second, you can wait until the heartbeat retrospective and ask team members to recall how they felt on each day of the iteration just completed. Either way, during the retrospective, the pattern provides inspiration for a team discussion of opportunities for improvement.

3.13.2 Examples

Figure 3.20 shows an example from the Munich-based DMC Group, from one of their retrospectives. The sticky notes across the bottom of the board contain ideas for discussion during the retrospective. The chart across the top is the emotional seismogram: it represents each team member's recollection of how he or she felt on each day of the iteration.

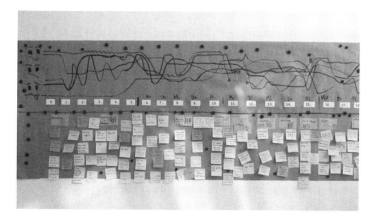

Figure 3.20   Emotional seismogram

When you can't use a Niko Niko calendar, an emotional seismogram can provide an alternative means of getting at team members' emotional state. It's weaker than the Niko Niko calendar in that it relies on people's memories of how they felt, rather than taking a real-time snapshot of people's feelings each day.

In my experience, people's memories of how they felt earlier in the iteration are strongly conditioned by the outcome of the iteration. In addition, an emotional seismogram is used during retrospectives as one mechanism among several to ferret out specific opportunities for improvement. In contrast, a Niko Niko calendar collects raw data that reveals trends over time. For these reasons, I suggest using a Niko Niko calendar whenever your team is willing to agree to it, and resorting to alternatives only when necessary.

3.14 *Metric: Happiness index*

Question(s) answered
- How do team members feel about working here?

Description
- A rough indication of team morale based on team members' subjective rating of their own feelings about the work environment

Value
- Can detect the emotional impact of organizational problems before the root causes make themselves evident
- Can detect a trend of falling morale in time to prevent team collapse

Dependencies

- Approach: any
- Process model: any
- Delivery mode: any

Success factors

- Best when used in an organizational culture that ensures safety when staff members express less-than-positive feelings about the workplace
- When used in an unsafe organizational culture, inputs to the happiness index should be anonymous.

3.14.1 When to use the happiness index

Use the happiness index when you want to get a sense of how team morale is evolving over time.

3.14.2 Mechanics

Ask team members to rate their own level of happiness. You can do this on a one-off basis when you want to take a reading of the team's emotional state, or you can make it a regular practice. In the latter case, take readings at a consistent interval: once a day, once a week, once per iteration, and so on. Then you can chart the changes in responses over time to see how the team is evolving or detect problems based on the emotional impact of those problems.

Here's an example of how the happiness index can work. Let's say you have a team of eight people, the team is using a time-boxed iterative process model, and team members have rated their happiness on a scale of 1 to 5 for several iterations (see figure 3.21).

A	B	C	D	E	F	G	H	I	J
1	Joseph	Amir	Sheila	Rhonda	Stanley	Alice	Rajesh	Hong	
1	3	5	1	3	5	2	3	2	
2	3	4	1	3	5	3	3	3	
3	4	3	3	1	1	2	3	2	
4	4	2	3	1	5	2	3	4	
5	3	2	3	1	1	3	3	3	
6	3	2	4	1	1	2	3	4	
7	2	2	3	1	5	3	3	2	
8	2	4	4	1	1	3	3	3	
9	3	4	3	1	5	2	3	2	
10	3	4	3	1	5	2	3	3	
Averages	3	3.2	2.8	1.4	3.4	2.4	3	2.8	2.75

Figure 3.21   Happiness index data

If you plot the individual responses, you get a fairly cluttered chart that gives you a visual sense of how team members' feelings changed over the course of these iterations, as shown in figure 3.22. From this, you can tell that individual team members feel very differently from one another about working here.

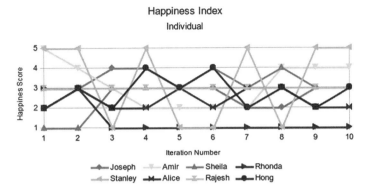

Figure 3.22   Happiness index: all the individual results

You can focus on one individual at a time if you want to see how their feelings are changing. Let's look at a few individual results. These examples are representative of common patterns you're likely to see when you use this metric. We'll start with the team member named Joseph (see figure 3.23).

Figure 3.23
Happiness index: Joseph

Joseph's feelings about work fluctuate around the midpoint of the scale. This is how most people feel about working in a typical corporate IT environment. Some days are better than others, but in general they feel more or less neutral about their work. Some aficionados of contemporary lightweight methods might see this as a problem; they tend to expect team members to remain highly engaged and excited at all times. In reality, people can't maintain a high level of emotional engagement without pause. It's exhausting!

Now consider Stanley (figure 3.24). Stanley appears to have a love-hate relationship with his work; he always scores his happiness at one extreme or the other. Is he emotionally unstable? Probably not. When asked to respond on a scale, many people tend to choose the minimum or maximum score. Chances are, his true feelings are more or less the same as Joseph's.

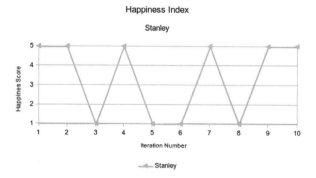

Figure 3.24
Happiness index: Stanley

Rhonda is a different story, as you can see in figure 3.25. You might want to have a private chat with Rhonda. Clearly, something about the work environment isn't meeting her needs. Based on her pattern of responses, my first guess would be that she was already having difficulties at work before she became part of this team. Joining the team may have given her a temporary morale boost; initially she was willing to give it a fair try, and she had a neutral attitude toward work. But the new team did not solve her problems.

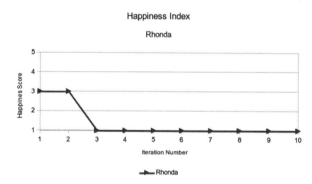

Figure 3.25
Happiness index: Rhonda

The situation is interesting because it may point to workplace issues that affect Rhonda negatively, or it may indicate the Omega Wolf pattern you saw with the Niko Niko calendar examples. The appropriate corrective action depends on the root cause. As usual, the metric doesn't tell you the root cause; it only raises a warning that there may be a problem.

Rajesh has quite a different pattern of responses, as shown in figure 3.26. Rajesh never seems to feel particularly good or bad about work. He's consistently neutral. This pattern usually means one of two things: either he derives professional satisfaction from activities other than his day job, or he prefers not to share his feelings and provides neutral responses no matter how he feels.

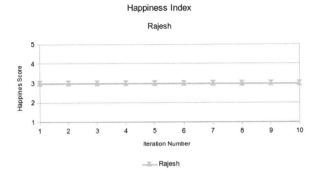

Figure 3.26
Happiness index: Rajesh

Individual responses are often less useful than the team average. If a team member is having problems, it's usually evident without using a metric like the happiness index. The team average may help identify patterns in the work flow or organizational constraints that drive down team morale. Let's look at the pattern for this team, shown in figure 3.27.

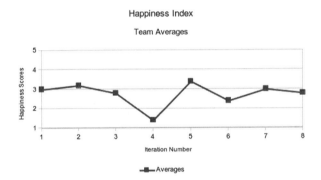

Figure 3.27
Happiness index: team averages

In this case, the team seems to be cruising along nicely most of the time. There's a dip in happiness in iteration 4. If you were to look at other metrics for the team, you would probably find that the dip correlates with the team's delivery performance in iteration 4. People's feelings about work often vary in direct proportion to their success. This may be true in part because people naturally prefer to perform well and to achieve their goals. In larger organizations particularly, it may be true in part because people fear negative performance appraisals.

In an organization of high trust, you'll see teams recover quickly from emotional dips like this. If the team doesn't recover quickly, and morale remains low even after the hiccup in performance is past, it may indicate that the organizational culture is toxic.

3.15 *Metric: Balls in bowls*

Question(s) answered
- How do team members feel about working here?

Description
- Gives a rough indication of team morale based on team members' subjective rating of their own feelings about the work environment

Value
- Can provide a simple point-in-time reading of team morale

Dependencies
- Approach: any
- Process model: any
- Delivery mode: any

Success factors
- Best when used in an organizational culture that ensures safety when staff members express less-than-positive feelings about the workplace
- Not advised when the organizational culture is unsafe, because anyone can see who places red balls in the container

3.15.1 *When to use the balls-in-bowls metric*

Use the balls-in-bowls metric when you want a quick check of team morale at a point in time.

3.15.2 *Mechanics*

This approach collects the same sort of information as a Niko Niko calendar or happiness index, but with low setup effort. It's a spot check; it isn't meant to collect data over time to develop trends.

Provide the team with enough balls that each team member has one. Place two bowls near the exit, and ask each team member to place their ball in one bowl or the other, where one bowl is for good and one is for bad. Don't offer any explanations.

Any variation that amounts to a good or bad choice will work as well. For instance, some teams use red and green cards or sticky notes. If no bowls are available, team members can place their cards on a table.

3.16 *Metric: Health and happiness*

Question(s) answered
- How do team members feel about their delivery performance and job satisfaction?

Description
- Provides a point-in-time indication of team members' subjective assessment of their own delivery performance (health) and job satisfaction (happiness). A series of observations can provide a trend in how the team feels about these factors over time. This metric was developed by ScrumMaster Kevin Davis.

Value
- Can raise a warning when improved delivery performance is achieved at the cost of team morale

- Can raise a warning when improved team morale doesn't lead to improved delivery performance
- Can indicate whether team members associate strong delivery performance with high job satisfaction
- Can indicate that the team is settling into a comfort zone without improving or maintaining delivery performance

Dependencies
- Approach: any
- Process model: any
- Delivery mode: any

Success factors
- In a safe organizational culture, team members can mark the chart openly, in full view of teammates. This can lead to constructive discussion of opportunities for improvement.
- In an unsafe organizational culture, a facilitator can collect anonymous scores for health and happiness and plot the points on the chart. This can lead to constructive team discussions without pointing at any individuals.

3.16.1 *When to use the health-and-happiness metric*

Data collection for this metric is normally done as a recurring team activity. If the team practices heartbeat retrospectives, include this as a brief activity in each retrospective. If the team doesn't use this practice, then schedule a brief team meeting at fixed intervals (say, every two weeks) for the activity.

3.16.2 *Mechanics*

The facilitator prepares a quadrant chart with two axes. The x-axis represents the team's happiness—that is, a subjective indication of how team members feel about working with the team. The y-axis represents the team's health—that is, team members' subjective sense of how effectively the team is delivering results. The basic chart looks something like figure 3.28.

Each team member places a mark on the chart that shows how they feel about the team's delivery performance and about their own work with the team as of that moment. In an environment characterized by high trust and transparency, the team

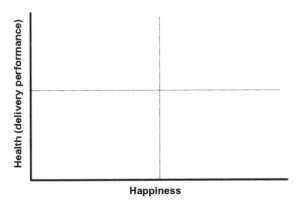

Figure 3.28   Health-and-happiness chart (empty)

can gather in front of the chart and place their marks openly. In an environment where trust is an issue, the facilitator can solicit anonymous input from the team and then place all the marks on the chart.

Once all the marks have been placed on the chart, the team engages in an open-ended discussion about the reasons people feel the way they do about the work. For example, figure 3.29 shows a chart for the arbitrary date April 9, after a hypothetical team has placed their marks.

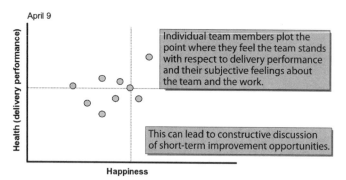

Figure 3.29   Health-and-happiness chart: April 9 (raw)

At some point in the discussion, the team reaches a consensus about their collective sense of team health and happiness and arrives at a single point (see figure 3.30). This becomes a data point to be added to historical health and happiness indices to provide a sense of how the team's morale is trending. In the shorter term, the discussion by which the team reaches consensus often yields useful insights, uncovers hidden problems, and improves team cohesion.

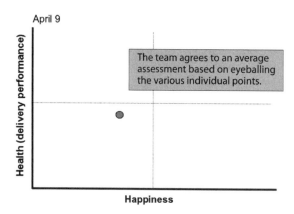

Figure 3.30   Health-and-happiness chart: April 9 (team average)

The facilitator (probably you, in view of the intended audience for this book) adds the data point for April 9 to the historical data from previous sessions, as shown in figure 3.31. With repeated input, the accumulated information shows how the team's subjective assessment of delivery performance and happiness changes over time (see figure 3.32).

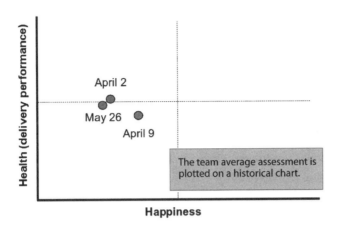

Figure 3.31   Health-and-happiness Chart (historical)

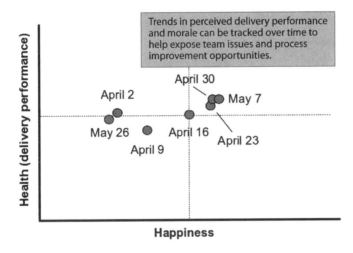

Figure 3.32   Health-and-happiness chart (long-term)

3.17   *Metric: Personality type profiles*

Question(s) answered

- How can team members with different personality types or cognitive styles communicate and collaborate effectively to achieve the common goals of the team?

Description

- Team members self-assess, or are assessed by an outside consultant, to determine their personality types or cognitive styles as defined by a particular model. They then learn a few practical ways they can communicate clearly and collaborate effectively with individuals who have different, and possibly conflicting, personality types or cognitive styles.

Value

- Can help the team gel into a cohesive, functioning unit

Dependencies

- Approach: any
- Process model: any
- Delivery mode: any

Success factors

- Best in conjunction with collaborative working styles, such as cross-functional teams working in the same team room

3.17.1 *When to use personality profiles*

Use personality profiles to help team members understand how to interact effectively with one another. For any team to function well, and particularly when the team is using a collaborative style of working, it's helpful for the team members to understand themselves and their teammates. This isn't to say that everyone has to become close friends or learn intimate secrets about one another; it only means you need to understand your own tendencies, the tendencies of your teammates, and concrete actions you can take to ensure that you're able to collaborate effectively.

Quite a few personality assessments are available. In the context of teamwork for software development, you aren't interested in a deep dive into everyone's psychological makeup; rather, you're interested in identifying team members' general tendencies in personal interaction. Understanding traits like dominance versus submissiveness, analytical thinking versus instinctive thinking, and so forth can help people learn how to communicate and collaborate effectively on the job.

General models designed for nonprofessional use are practical for this purpose. Many companies use DiSC profiles, the Myers-Briggs Type Indicator (MBTI), or Personalysis. StrengthsFinder is another commercial assessment that can help team members understand how to interact with one another effectively, although it isn't a personality profile as such. These products can be helpful, provided you remember their limitations. None is scientifically rigorous, and none is used by healthcare professionals in their work with patients.

In-depth coverage of these models is out of scope of this book. I have no particular recommendations in this area. The key point is that team members have some way of understanding how they communicate and how their individual styles of communication are received by teammates who have different personality types.

Friction between team members is often a cause of software delivery problems. When people make assumptions about their own communication style and those of their teammates, misunderstandings often lead to friction. By improving your understanding of yourself as well as your teammates, you can avoid misunderstandings. That's the reason I consider this a pragmatic metric to support improvement.

3.17.2 *Anti-patterns*

Understanding how different personality types interact can be helpful, but it can also lead to certain undesirable behaviors.

AN EXCUSE TO AVOID COLLABORATION

Be alert for team members who want to use the results of the personality assessment as an excuse to avoid collaborating with others who have different profiles. Contemporary software-development methods usually call for collaboration on a level that hasn't been the norm in IT work for most of the past several decades. It's natural for people to resist shifting from individual work to collaborative work. Expect to see this behavior especially with respect to pair programming and cross-disciplinary collaboration (for instance, business analysts and testers working directly together to create executable test cases that express requirements).

It's true that some personality types naturally conflict. When this is the case, it becomes your professional responsibility to learn how to collaborate effectively with the other person. It isn't an excuse to avoid collaboration.

EXPLOITATION

Many years ago, William Oncken came up with a time-management model he called the Molecule of Management (http://www.onckencorp.com/molecule.htm.) The basic idea is that no matter the size of your organization, you personally interact with just four types of entities: your boss, your internal peers, your external peers, and your subordinates. Each of these has a unique role with respect to you, and you need to learn specific techniques to work effectively with each.

Many people who received training in this model began to use their knowledge to manipulate others in their organizations. I've seen people induce others to happily perform nearly all their work. This wasn't the intent of the model, but it's often employed in this way.

Personality profiles like MBTI and DiSC can be abused in much the same way. Clever team members may learn to manipulate others by pressing their buttons. This is counterproductive to the team's goals, because it tends to reduce the effective delivery capacity of the team as a whole.

3.18 *Summary*

This chapter introduced several metrics that can help monitor the effects of process-improvement efforts. You learned that overgeneralized assumptions about how people are motivated often cause improvement efforts to flounder and can cause measurements of improvements to be inaccurate.

You learned about anti-patterns that can occur when using metrics to assess the effectiveness of improvement efforts. You also saw how certain metrics can be used both for steering and for process improvement.

The chapter also discussed the fact that technical and human metrics can be used to help with process improvement. But they aren't typically helpful with steering, and they aren't usually reported outside the team.

Putting the metrics to work

This chapter covers

- Applying multiple metrics to expose potential areas of improvement
- Using patterns and trends to point to delivery problems

In this chapter, you'll see how you can gain deeper insight into a situation by using multiple metrics, and multiple types of metrics, in concert. Trends in any single metric can highlight delivery issues, but can just as easily provide a false positive. When you overlay trends in multiple metrics, false positives tend to become obvious, and you can catch problems early.

So far, you've learned about the purpose, function, basic mechanics, and potential abuses of several metrics, and how your development approach, process model, and delivery mode influence your choice of metrics. You've seen that a single point-in-time observation offers little useful information and that you need to develop observation trends over time.

No single metric gives you all the information you need to keep your work on track or to recognize areas of improvement. When you overlay trends in multiple metrics, you can get a better sense of what's happening. Even then, metrics won't directly tell you the root causes of a problem; they'll only indicate when reality diverges from expectations or exceeds limits you've defined as "normal." It's still up to you to discover root causes and determine appropriate actions. The more information you have, the better your chances of success in doing so.

Let's consider a few examples. These are patterns I've seen in the field time and again.

4.1 Pattern 1: Periodic refactoring iterations

In this case, a development team exhibits a recurring pattern of erratic delivery performance. Let's assume they're using a time-boxed iterative process model in which they deliver production-ready solution increments in each iteration. The pattern is that they deliver well at first, but then gradually slow down until they must devote an entire iteration to cleaning up the code. Then the pattern repeats.

Let's see how this pattern appears when you overlay trends in several metrics:

- *Velocity*—The quantity of production-ready software completed in each iteration, expressed as story points
- *Cyclomatic complexity*—The number of linearly independent paths through the source code
- *Automated test coverage*—How much of the code is exercised by automated test cases
- *Niko Niko calendar*—The general mood of team members

Figure 4.1 shows how the pattern manifests in the four selected metrics. The figure overlays the four metrics on a common timeline.

Notice that the metrics shown in the figure represent different categories of measurement. You're looking at the team's delivery performance through multiple different lenses. This approach often enables a richer understanding of what's happening than can be achieved using any single metric or single type of metric.

The team starts by delivering results at their normal level of performance. Gradually, the quality of the code deteriorates until it reaches a point that is unmanageable. In order to continue development, the team must dedicate an iteration to cleaning up the code. During that time, no progress is made in building the product. After the code has been cleaned up, the pattern repeats. Unfortunately, the example isn't speculative—it represents an all-too-common pattern in industry.

Usually, this pattern occurs when a team feels real or perceived pressure to deliver as quickly as possible, and damn the consequences. They cut corners to try to work faster. Instead, they slow themselves down. They pile `if/else` blocks on top of other `if/else` blocks. They copy and paste snippets of code and leave remnants throughout the code base. They skimp on automated test cases. These practices result in more defects, which cause the team to spend proportionally more time identifying and fixing bugs than on value-add development work. Lacking sufficient test coverage, the defect-resolution activities take longer than they should.

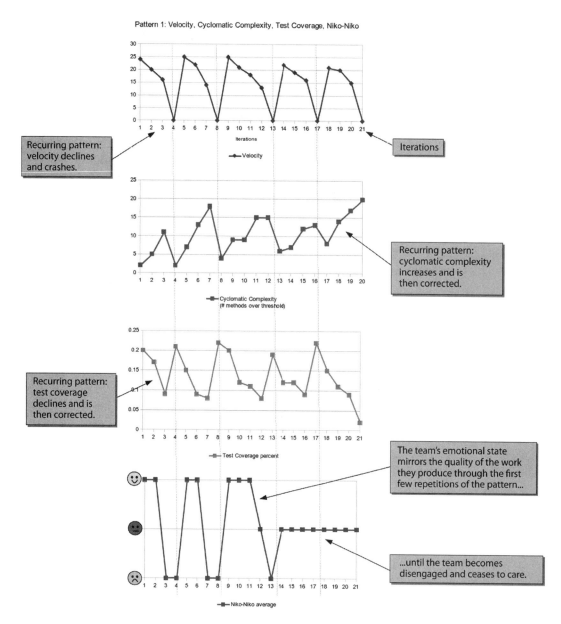

Figure 4.1   Pattern 1: velocity, cyclomatic complexity, automated test coverage, and Niko Niko calendar

It's unsurprising to see the correlations between velocity, cyclomatic complexity, and automated test coverage. You would see predictable correlations with throughput, cycle time, and process cycle efficiency (PCE) as well. Notice, however, the way the Niko Niko calendar changes as the pattern repeats. After a while, the team becomes disengaged; they become a zombie team. The stress and monotony of the periodic refactoring iterations, during which stakeholders are displeased at the lack of progress, and the unrelenting pressure to work faster and faster with no opportunity to address the root causes of the problem, eventually wear them down.

The zombie-team problem often leads to further delivery issues. It's likely that turnover will increase and that the company will begin to earn a negative reputation in the local labor market that makes it increasingly difficult to fill vacant positions. This can lead to a downward spiral for the organization's ability to deliver.

When you overlay graphics of these metrics on a timeline, the result is a powerful visual representation of the impact of policies that are inhibiting effective delivery of valuable software. It's a much more effective message than telling management and stakeholders that the team feels pressure—they would say that pressure is a normal part of the job. Metrics convey a message they can relate to on a gut level.

The Niko Niko calendar may seem to be a soft metric, but in a situation like this it can expose deeper problems than process metrics and technical metrics. Once the team becomes disengaged, their disengagement becomes the primary cause of poor delivery performance. Until that issue has been addressed, changes in process or in technical practices will have little or no effect.

CORRECTIVE ACTION

This pattern usually occurs when a team feels pressure to deliver as rapidly as possible (regardless of whether the pressure is real or perceived), and when they believe the best way to deliver quickly is to cut corners with respect to technical practices. In general, corrective action involves helping the team understand the business value of delivering clean code in a predictable and sustainable way, and helping the team learn (if necessary) and adopt generally accepted good software development practices. As the team makes progress with these corrective actions, expect the metrics to start shaping up, as shown in figure 4.2.

The new pattern in velocity shows an initial reduction in delivery as the team starts to make improvements in the code base. Velocity climbs until it reaches the team's norm, where it stabilizes.

The corresponding pattern in cyclomatic complexity shows the number of offending methods starting high and gradually falling to a reasonable level as the team refactors code to simplify complicated branch structures. As the team cleans up the code base, they add automated tests. In the course of a few iterations, they bring the level of test coverage up to an acceptable range.

At the same time, the Niko Niko calendar exhibits a normal trend as the team adopts new work practices. Initially, morale is low because the team is uncertain about the new technical practices they're adopting, and because they may be less than fully confident in management's claims that delivery pressure will be relaxed to enable better technical practices. Once they begin to see the positive impact of the changes they're making, their morale improves to a normal pattern, shifting mostly between positive and neutral.

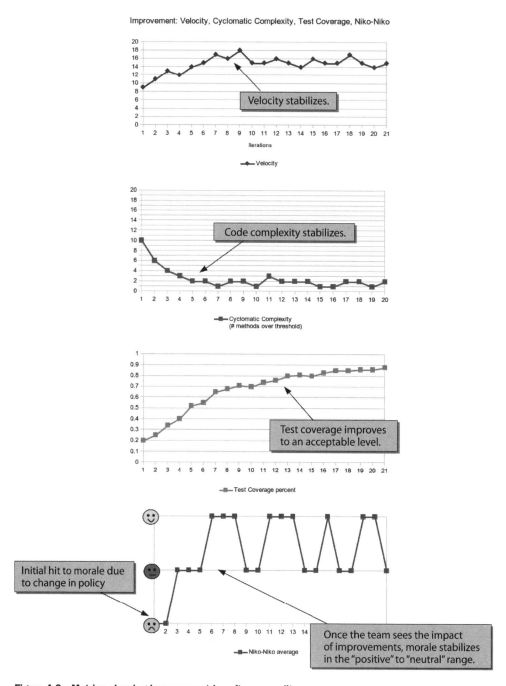

Figure 4.2   Metrics showing improvement in software quality

4.2   *Pattern 2: Velocity looks good, but little is delivered*

Given a time-boxed iterative process model, velocity is meant to reflect the quantity of production-ready software a team delivers in each iteration. In many organizations, it can be challenging to deliver any production-ready software in a short time. Typical inhibiting factors are discussed next.

ORGANIZATIONAL STRUCTURE

In a business-application software development and support organization, it's generally a good idea to align people and resources with the flow of work necessary to deliver results. In Lean thinking, the idea is expressed as aligning value-producing activities with the value stream. Many corporate IT organizations define teams around technical assets rather than along value streams. For instance, they may have a team responsible for supporting IBM WebSphere AS, another responsible for supporting Oracle RDBMS, another for supporting an enterprise service bus (ESB), another responsible for configuring servers, and on and on. To complete any given development project, several of these component teams must be engaged to perform small amounts of work on behalf of the project team. This communication structure causes delays in delivery.

GOVERNANCE PROCESSES

Business enterprises of any appreciable size try to carry out their work in a reliable way. They have standards and guidelines to be followed in many areas of work, including network security, user-interface branding, accessibility. In addition, many companies are subject to government regulations of one kind or another. Software delivery processes often deal with these requirements at the end of the delivery chain by including review and approval steps before any software is permitted into the production environment. This approach makes it challenging to deliver software according to the time-boxed iterative model. Most or all of these activities can be folded into the delivery pipeline at earlier points in the process, allowing product to flow more smoothly to production.

RESOURCE CONSTRAINTS

It sometimes seems as if large corporate IT departments are willing to spend copious amounts of money on their production resources, but they're reluctant to provide adequate resources for development and (especially) testing. I've often seen teams that are ready to move forward with the current iteration's work but can't get immediate access to a test environment, or must wait for another group to condition test data (another indicator of organizational structure problems). To support incremental delivery, development teams must have control of the resources they need to deliver fully tested software in each iteration. This may include the ability to define and run virtual machines, to stand up physical servers, to configure and launch mainframe systems such as CICS, and to create and load databases.

MANUAL DELIVERY PIPELINE

Competitive pressure and the pace of change are steadily increasing, and time to market has become one of the key business drivers for software delivery. Practices such as A/B testing require the ability to deploy small changes in applications at any time, without delay, in order to respond to customer demand. Yet many large IT organizations still depend on manual methods for building, packaging, testing, deploying, and monitoring the software they develop. One cause of erratic delivery may be the delays created by a reliance on manual methods to pull software through the delivery pipeline.

CHARACTERISTICS OF DEVELOPMENT TOOLS AND OTHER PRODUCTS IN THE ENVIRONMENT

Many large IT organizations have dependencies on third-party software packages for mission-critical functions. To make a modification to an application, a team may have to make configuration changes or custom modifications to more than one third-party product, such as an extract, transform, load (ETL) package; a customer relationship management (CRM) package; a business rules engine; an enterprise service bus (ESB); and so forth. An issue already mentioned is that each of these packages may be supported by a separate team. In addition, some packages may have been designed in an era when the largest IT cost was the computer hardware and when lead times of two years or more were considered normal and acceptable. Those products are designed to support multiple applications within a single container and to share precious hardware resources efficiently. They're designed to be the sole inhabitant of the universe and not to function as one component of a larger system, having to play nicely with other components. They aren't designed to support frequent, numerous, rapid, small changes by multiple teams at the same time. Their very architecture inhibits a team's ability to deliver incrementally.

PROCESS STRUCTURE

Even when a time-boxed iterative model is used, it's common for the process followed in each iteration to be linear. Some people refer to this as an *iterative waterfall process.* When this is a cause of erratic delivery, it can be mitigated by limiting work in process (WIP) and encouraging the team to complete one (or a few) work items at a time, collaborating across roles, rather than batching the work items and working through traditional development phases.

FUNCTIONAL SILOS

In the past 15 years or so, there's been a move toward poly-skilled IT professionals. Catch phrases like *generalizing specialist* and *T-shaped people* have made the rounds. Formal job descriptions have lagged behind this trend, and longstanding assumptions about the need for functional specialization in IT have been slow to change. Cross-functional development teams using a time-boxed iterative process model tend to consist of specialists in various areas rather than poly-skilled individuals who can perform several kinds of tasks on behalf of the team. Demand for particular skills tends to wax and wane over the course of a project. On a team of specialists, this causes some individuals to be overloaded and others to be idle at any given time. You must consider the fact that people choose a specialization because it interests them, and they want to spend most of their time in that area. Most IT professionals don't *want* to perform all kinds of different tasks on a routine basis. Even so, when demand for skills shifts, it's useful for team members to be able to pick up some of the work outside their individual area of specialization from time to time.

PERFORMANCE APPRAISALS

I often visit organizations where management says all the right things about cross-functional collaboration and a team-oriented approach to work, but the formal performance-appraisal guidelines strongly emphasize individual accomplishment over collaboration. Combined with a "stack ranking" approach to workforce management, the individually focused appraisal guidelines cause people to protect themselves at the expense of their colleagues. They may hide information that might make them look bad. They may see a problem coming and say nothing to prevent it, so that they can later fix the problem and emerge as a hero. They may remain silent when a colleague makes a poor decision, because the result will benefit them in the rank-and-yank scheme. You probably won't see any glaring, dramatic examples of such behavior; but the net effect of thousands of small events introduces friction in the delivery pipeline that results in erratic team performance and delays in delivery, even when individual contributors appear to be doing everything right.

SCARCE SPECIALISTS

Some of the activities involved in IT work genuinely require narrow-and-deep specialists. A generalist can't do *everything* well. Usually, such individuals are both rare and expensive, and organizations have only a few of them on staff. Their services are in demand by many development teams simultaneously, and it isn't practical to assign one of them to each development team for the full duration of a project. The situation creates a queuing problem. There will be a delay each time a team requests services from a rare specialist. You can't eliminate this delay completely. By making the issue visible, you may be able to find ways to manage the queuing problem more efficiently and minimize the impact on delivery performance.

MEETINGS

Many companies begin life as startups, hoping for success. When success comes, it often comes quickly. As the company increases sales, increases production, and grows market share, things can be hectic. More and more people are affected by business decisions, and they all need information. No one pauses to reason through problems or determine how best to provide people with exactly the information they need at exactly the time they need it. What usually happens is that meetings proliferate. People schedule meetings to discuss every decision, and they invite more and more attendees. When technical personnel are involved in these meetings, it destroys their productivity. Technical work requires long periods of focus. A single meeting scheduled midmorning and another mid-afternoon eliminate all opportunities for extended focus for the entire day. People need to learn how to identify the meetings where their attendance is really necessary and to decline other meeting invitations. A simple expedient is to block out periods on your calendar for uninterrupted work.

TIME MANAGEMENT

Above and beyond scheduled meetings, many technical team members have difficulty managing their time. They tend to function on an interrupt-driven basis. They often end up juggling many unfinished tasks as they try to address every fire and every new request immediately. The idea of limiting WIP has already been mentioned; it applies to this problem, as well. Teams get more done when they try to finish things one by one than when they start everything at once and juggle many tasks. There are methods that can help you manage incoming work requests in a reasonable way; for example, Kanban helps with this issue (see *Kanban in Action* by Marcus Hammarberg and Joakim Sundén, Manning, 2014).

INDIVIDUAL AND TEAM TECHNICAL PRACTICES

Software development teams develop software. For that reason, people usually assume that any delay in delivery must be due to poor software-development practices. They try to address delivery delays by introducing new technical practices or by sending team members to training classes. These remedies rarely have any measurable effect on delivery effectiveness. The specific development practices a team employs usually have less impact on delivery effectiveness than the previous issues. That said, technical practices can have an effect. Teams that don't use version control must pause from time to time to re-create lost code or resolve conflicts in different copies of the code. Teams that don't practice continuous integration must pause to integrate components manually. Teams that don't use automated testing must pause to test the basic functionality of their code manually. Teams that don't drive code from executable examples must pause to investigate the causes of defects and repair the code. Teams that don't keep their code clean as they go along, using a technique known as *incremental refactoring*, gradually accumulate design debt that makes the application increasingly difficult to understand and to modify safely; it can even cause an application to become unmaintainable long before its intended production lifetime. Because organizational impediments have such a powerful negative impact on delivery performance, many professional developers are unaware that their technical practices could be improved. Even if they could be doing substantially more and higher-quality work, they're able to produce results quickly enough for their organizations to consume the changes, but this may only be because the organization isn't particularly efficient.

GAMING VELOCITY

When teams fear negative consequences for failing to show steady velocity, they may respond to these issues by softening the definition of velocity so they can avoid punishment for failing to deliver something in every iteration. This can be problematic, because you want metrics to make problems visible as a first step toward correcting them. When metrics are used in a way that hides problems, you have no basis for improvement.

Why would a team falsify their velocity?

If velocity is meant to help teams, then why would a team game the numbers? Most often, the reason is that the organization expects teams to report their velocity to management. Many managers don't understand that velocity isn't comparable across teams, and they want to use it to rank teams and personnel.

Ideally, velocity is a metric useful to a single team and isn't reported to anyone outside the team. It's a tool to help a self-organizing team manage its own work flow. As soon as you share velocity beyond the team, you risk creating fear within the team that the numbers will be used against them at performance-appraisal time. That can destroy the metric's usefulness as an early warning of delivery problems. Other metrics are available that external stakeholders can use to gauge progress.

One of the ways teams game velocity is by manipulating their user-story sizing or estimation. They adjust user-story sizes up or down as necessary to make it appear as if they're achieving high velocity. They assign story points to work other than user stories so they can claim completion of work items more frequently than would be possible if they waited for each user story to be fully and properly finished.

Another way to game velocity is to organize planned work into items that aren't proper user stories. A user story represents a thin vertical slice of functionality that can be tested and demonstrated, even if it amounts to less functionality than you would put into production without other pieces in place. Teams often treat small tasks as if they were user stories so they can assign points to the tasks. They decompose the work horizontally, by architectural layer, rather than create vertical slices, and they claim points for each separate portion of development—for instance, database changes, middleware changes, and front-end changes. They divide user stories that have external dependencies into multiple parts so they can claim each part as complete individually, without losing credit for work while awaiting results from external groups. The focus is on getting credit for story points, rather than on delivering working software that has business value for stakeholders.

Because the team is gaming velocity, the problem may not be apparent in a velocity chart or burn chart alone. When you combine velocity observations with other metrics, you can expose this sort of issue. Let's combine the following metrics:

- *Velocity*—The quantity of production-ready software completed in each iteration, expressed as story points (in this case, incorrectly calculated)
- *Running tested features (RTF)*—The number of software features running in a production or staging environment with all automated tests passing
- *Earned business value (EBV)*—The amount of relative business value delivered to date
- *Throughput*—The number of features delivered to production per release

Consider the pattern in these four metrics shown in figure 4.3. It appears that velocity is stable, which is what you want to see. But for some reason the team isn't building up more functionality in the automated test environment, as reflected by the trend in RTF. If the team was delivering results steadily, then you would expect to see RTF climb steadily.

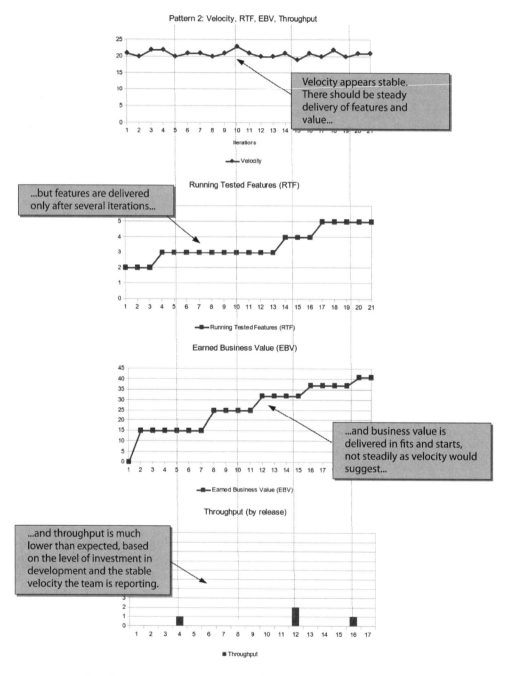

Figure 4.3   Pattern 2: velocity, RTF, EBV, and throughput

EBV provides another indication that velocity isn't showing true performance. Teams ought to focus on delivering the highest-value features early and lower-value features later. EBV normally forms an S-curve shape that mirrors this. Instead, here you see occasional delivery of business value, with several intervening iterations when no business value is produced.

The erratic throughput indicates that the team isn't delivering features as steadily as their velocity chart suggests. The team is working steadily and putting in a lot of time in development, and yet deploying relatively little functionality in each release. In addition, throughput is erratic, which makes it difficult to have confidence in any delivery plan.

Due to the popularity of velocity, many teams depend on that single metric to gauge progress. This example shows that when velocity is gamed, you may not see red flags that point to potential improvements in delivery performance. By using additional measures in conjunction with velocity, you can expose problems that otherwise may be hidden.

CORRECTIVE ACTION

Metrics don't tell you exactly what to do to correct problems; they only raise a flag to call your attention to situations where reality is diverging from expectations. The team can create an opportunity to see delivery problems by tracking their true velocity instead of playing games to make the velocity chart look normal. They can craft proper user stories, even if the stories can't be completed in the span of a single iteration, as per the general definition of a time-boxed iterative process model. They can size user stories according to their honest sense of relative size, rather than adjust points to make the velocity chart look good. Then they can let the numbers fall where they may so that delivery problems become visible. At that point, it becomes a root-cause analysis.

Let's say the team in this example allows velocity to reflect reality, and they identify specific changes they can make that will improve delivery performance. As the team makes progress with corrective actions, the metrics start shaping up, as shown in figure 4.4.

The immediate effect is that velocity drops dramatically. If velocity has been shared outside the team, then stakeholders will be interested to know why this is happening. Fortunately, it's easy to explain. Stakeholders are unlikely to be happy just because the velocity chart looked good; they have been the direct recipients of poor delivery. The previous trend in velocity was false, and now you intend to address the root causes of poor delivery performance. Stakeholders ought to take this as good news.

Initially, there's no improvement in the other metrics. At this early stage, there will be a temptation to abandon the improvement initiative and return to the old practice of gaming velocity. The other metrics haven't changed because the team hasn't done anything to improve delivery performance. All they've done is make their true velocity visible for the first time. If they want to see their velocity stabilize for the right reasons, then they must find and address the root causes of poor delivery performance.

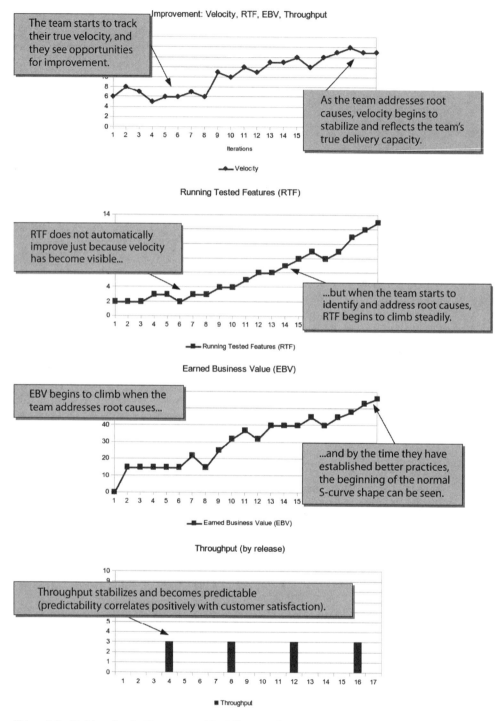

Figure 4.4   Metrics showing improvement in delivery performance

This example shows how the metrics change once the team begins to address root causes. The trend in velocity changes. It begins at the true level, which is much worse than was reported previously, and climbs to reflect the team's true norm once they begin to make improvements. The team's actual norm is lower than their previous false reading, but this isn't a bad thing because it represents true performance. Planning predictability will improve.

Both RTF and EBV begin to show steady growth instead of remaining flat for several iterations at a time. Toward the end of the sample period, EBV is showing the leftmost end of an S-curve shape, which indicates delivery of business value as per expectations for this sort of delivery process.

The most positive indicator is that throughput has stabilized. The team has demonstrated reliable delivery of three features per release for a span of three consecutive releases. Predictability correlates positively with stakeholder satisfaction. This improvement is likely to have a domino effect that the team will appreciate, leading to increased trust on the part of stakeholders and, based on that trust, increased autonomy for the team.

4.3 Pattern 3: Linear workflow packaged in time-boxed iterations

Basic iterative processes don't require any particular work to be completed within the span of a single iteration. Nor do they require each iteration to be the same length. The process can be structured in any way that makes sense in the local context. The process may be structured such that something usable is delivered in each iteration. Alternatively, one iteration can be dedicated to gathering requirements, the next to system design, the next two or three to building the code, the next to testing, and the next to deployment.

Time-boxed iterative processes like the ones that have gained popularity since the early 2000s are a bit more rigorous. They call for production-ready solution increments to be delivered in each iteration, and for the iterations to be the same length. Often, companies adopt a time-boxed iterative process model while retaining traditional assumptions about process structure. When they use a metric that depends on the time-boxed iterative model, like velocity, they find that the metric doesn't quite fit their process.

Consider the case when a linear process is chopped into iterations. There's no harm in using a basic iterative model this way, although there's no benefit, either. But when the organization believes it's using a time-boxed process, this approach is pointless, because there's no way to deliver production-ready solution increments in each iteration when following a linear development process.

Why use time-boxed iterations with a linear process?

If there's no benefit in using time-boxed iterations with a linear process, why do organizations do it? In the past 15 years, many organizations have adopted time-boxed iterative processes for software delivery. Results have been mixed, for a variety of reasons. The success stories are compelling, and organizations that wish to improve software delivery performance are eager to try methods that seem promising. They tend to get excited about the success stories while overlooking the lessons to be learned from other attempts.

The typical anti-pattern is that organizations create the outward appearance of a time-boxed iterative process without making the deeper changes necessary to realize value from it. They establish collaborative team work spaces; decorate the walls with tactile workflow-visualization tools, colorful posters, and upbeat slogans; divide the calendar into ostensible iterations; dutifully perform the ceremonies called for by their selected methodology; and adopt metrics that apply to time-boxed iterative processes, of which velocity is the most popular and the most widely abused.

Meanwhile, the organization forms teams around technical assets instead of along value streams; it retains job descriptions aligned with traditional functional silos; it measures performance by focusing on utilization instead of throughput; it appraises employee performance on an individual basis, in effect pitting team members against one another; it assumes software can only be developed by following a predefined series of steps in sequence; it invests heavily in up-front analysis and design to define a fixed scope, schedule, and budget for each project; it neglects to adopt technical practices that enable incremental delivery; and it treats the entire improvement initiative as strictly an IT matter, failing to engage business stakeholders. Then the organization wonders why the expected benefits of time-boxed iterative development don't materialize.

"We tried that. It didn't work."

In the example, a linear process is divided into time-boxed iterations. The linear process comprises a Requirements iteration, a Design iteration, three Code iterations, a Test iteration, and a Harden & Deploy iteration. After three repetitions of those iterations, software is released to production. Because velocity only counts for completed work items, no story points are earned until a release occurs. If velocity is tracked correctly in this case, it should look something like figure 4.5.

This is an obvious divergence from the time-boxed iterative process model, which calls for the delivery of a production-ready solution increment in each iteration. You may wonder why anyone would consider this sort of pattern acceptable. Human nature leads us to accept the status quo as normal. We tend not to see whatever usually happens as a problem. We sometimes assume that whatever usually happens is inevitable. Teams that fall into that mindset can look at a velocity chart like the one in figure 4.5 and see nothing wrong.

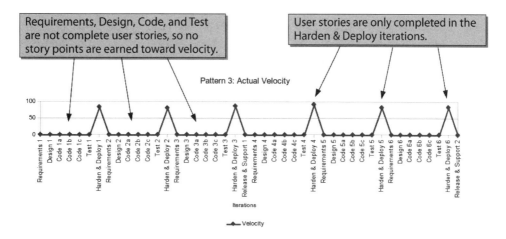

Figure 4.5   Velocity chart for a linear process carried through a series of iterations

When people *do* see something wrong, their response isn't necessarily to investigate and correct the root causes. Often, teams deal with this pattern by softening the definition of a user story so that they can claim credit for completing each step in the linear process. They create requirements stories, design stories, test stories, and so forth. Of course, none of these represents a vertical slice of functionality that can be tested and demonstrated; the team hasn't fixed the root cause of the problem. They've merely made the problem harder to see. Figure 4.6 shows such a velocity chart.

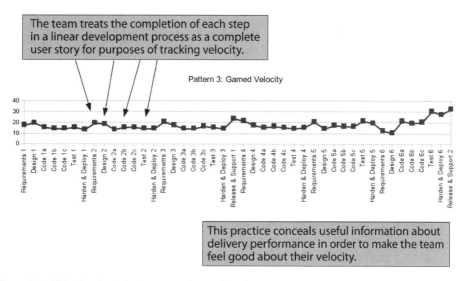

Figure 4.6   Velocity chart that treats each step in a linear process as a complete user story

You can make the problem more visible by tracking cycle time and lead time in addition to velocity. There's no need to chart the cycle time in this case, because it will be equal to the time required to prepare a production-ready solution increment. In this example, that means seven iterations. If you assume the iterations are two weeks long, and you assume 40-hour weeks with no holidays or other variations, then the cycle time for every user story is 560 hours. The team releases after every three sets of seven iterations. Thus the lead time, also known as *time-to-market* or *concept-to-cash* time, is 42 weeks. When you add in holidays, sick days, interruptions such as production support issues, the impact of employee turnover, and other real-world factors, it becomes clear that this process can deliver a solution about once a year. That is a far cry from the expectations management and stakeholders probably had when they decided to adopt a time-boxed linear process.

The apparently stable velocity may cause teams to feel complacent about delivery performance. When you also consider cycle time and lead time, it becomes clear that velocity isn't telling you the whole story. By exposing these issues through appropriate metrics, you can provide information to support recommendations for positive change.

CORRECTIVE ACTION

This pattern may result from any number of different factors, and from the interaction of multiple organizational forces and team practices. A detailed treatment of possible root causes is beyond the scope of this book. Metrics generally can't tell us the root cause of a problem. Indeed, metrics don't even tell us whether a situation is a problem at all. Metrics can raise a flag when something isn't happening according to expectations. The action we take, if any, depends on our context and goals.

4.4   *Pattern 4: Erratic velocity but stable delivery*

This pattern is the reverse of pattern 2. Rather than stable velocity combined with poor delivery, you see erratic velocity combined with stable delivery. Let's say velocity and the release-level burn chart look like figure 4.7.

The burn chart indicates the team is delivering software at a fairly steady rate. As is often the case, this team has a target velocity (yes, that's an error, but it's a common situation), and their actual performance is close to the ideal. It would be easy to accept the status quo and keep moving, possibly with a slight schedule slippage toward the end. Most organizations do just that, project after project.

The failure to align with the ideal trend line is neither good nor bad; the ideal line is useful only as a conversation starter with stakeholders. Velocity is a trailing indicator only and an empirical measure only. It can never function as a target.

People who are inexperienced with lightweight, adaptive methods may make the wrong assumptions based on the release burn chart. It appears as if the team is performing below expectations, if you take the ideal trend line to represent expected delivery performance. You might assume that you need to hire or reassign people to join the team, so that the team can keep up with the workload. This can be a dangerous

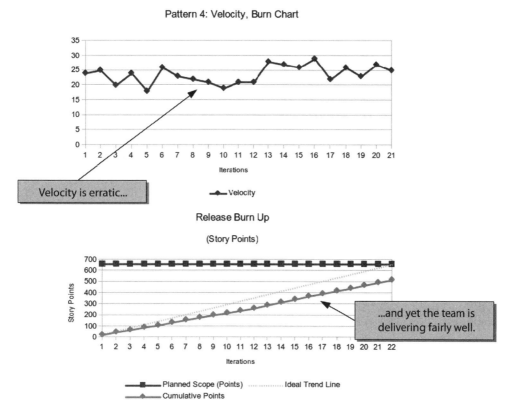

Figure 4.7 Velocity and release burn

assumption for a couple of reasons. First, the ideal trend line is only a discussion point, not an expectation based on any sort of analysis of the team's delivery capacity. Second, several other common issues are more likely to cause erratic velocity. It could be worse to try to solve a problem you don't have than to leave things as they are.

The *variation* in velocity is a red flag. It suggests the team may be struggling on some level. Anything might be happening at ground level. Is the team using technical practices that cause technical debt to accumulate in the code base? Is the team overloaded with work? Is the team's morale in decline? Are there external dependencies that cause the team to put work items on hold while they wait for turnaround from other teams or external suppliers? Each potential cause of erratic velocity calls for different corrective action. You need to find out exactly what's happening before you can decide on a course of action.

Let's take a closer look at how the work is flowing in each iteration. Figure 4.8 shows the daily iteration burn charts for the first four iterations.

The closer view of the workflow shows that the team doesn't complete many work items until late in each iteration. At that point, they rush to complete as much of the planned work as possible before the time box expires. The metrics have done their job; you now have a starting point for root-cause analysis.

A variety of causes can lead to this delivery pattern. Following are some examples.

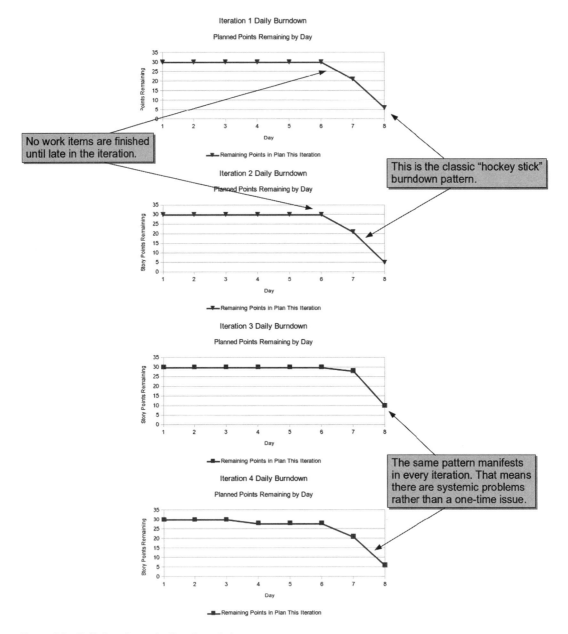

Figure 4.8   Daily burndowns for iterations 1–4

ORGANIZATIONAL STRUCTURE

Teams may be organized around technical assets rather than aligned with value streams or product lines. When this is the case, any single piece of work has to be touched by several teams before it can be completed—a database team, an architecture team, a UX team, a security team, a test-data provisioning team, and so on. Each work item comes to a halt at every point in the development process when the team has an external dependency. The root cause (organizational structure) may be outside the team's direct control, but they can use metrics to raise awareness of the problem with management. In the meantime, the team can negotiate service-level agreements (SLAs) with other teams on which they have dependencies, to help them plan their work in a predictable way.

FLOW MANAGEMENT

The team may be in the habit of starting every planned work item on the first day of each iteration and then juggling many active tasks simultaneously. In Lean terms, the work that's been started but not yet finished is called *work-in-process inventory*. When WIP is high, the rate of delivery slows because the team repeatedly experiences context-switching events as they juggle many work items. For this reason, WIP inventory is one of the basic forms of waste in Lean thinking. The team can manage WIP without anyone else's permission or assistance.

BATCH-ORIENTED THINKING

High WIP is sometimes a consequence of batch-oriented thinking. The basic time-boxed iterative model calls for delivery of a planned set of user stories in each iteration. It doesn't explicitly call for continuous delivery throughout the iteration. Many people tend to assume that this means delivering everything on the last day of the iteration is fine. It's useful to remember that time-boxed processes were designed as an improvement over linear and basic iterative processes. Linear processes are no longer the norm in software development organizations, and it's appropriate for you to look for improvements beyond the time-boxed model. Continuous delivery has already become a competitive edge for software organizations, and it's on its way to becoming an expected baseline. Even without thinking ahead to a continuous-delivery model, it's clear that waiting until the end of the iteration to finish the work has not enabled the team to meet delivery expectations, per the burn chart.

FUNCTIONAL SILOS

Many organizations form cross-functional teams when they first embrace lightweight methods, but don't change their assumption that software development has to be performed by functional specialists. Often, the result is a series of hand-offs within each time-boxed iteration. Functional specialists complete their part of the work and pass an interim artifact (typically, documentation) to the next functional specialist in line. The hockey-stick pattern can result when a business analyst performs analysis of all the user stories in plan during the first couple of days of the iteration, then a programmer writes the code, then a tester tests the code, and so forth. No user story can be deemed complete until the key stakeholder accepts delivery of functional, tested software. This can only occur at the end of the iteration, because it takes several days for a work item to pass through the entire series of hand-offs. The team can correct this problem by changing the way functional specialists interact in the course of completing the work. They can support their own efforts in this area by limiting WIP, as well. When team members with different specialties collaborate directly on one or two items at a time, the team as a whole can complete more work items in the course of an iteration.

TECHNICAL PRACTICES

The team may be able to adjust technical practices in ways that reduce the friction in getting the work done. For example, requirements may be written in such a way that programmers and testers must parse them and tease out the details. Typically, they don't understand the requirements in the same way that business analysts intended, and a certain amount of delay and rework ensues.

When requirements include specific, concrete, testable sample scenarios, then all team members have a good chance of reaching a shared understanding. Similarly, when programmers are working from testable examples, they can ensure that their code causes all the sample scenarios to pass. With those practices in place, testers can spend proportionally more time on value-add exploratory testing than on routine, repetitive validation or checking.

Simple things like using a common domain language throughout all project artifacts, following generally accepted software development principles, driving code directly from automated test cases, and close collaboration within and between functional specialties go a long way toward keeping the work flowing smoothly and avoiding misunderstandings. This helps the team get all the way to done without unpleasant surprises toward the end of the process.

Programmers can help keep the code base clean as they make modifications, by refactoring the code incrementally as they work rather than allowing design debt to accumulate. This prevents the code from becoming unmanageable over time and helps the team move work items through the delivery process smoothly.

HABITS

Through experience, we all adopt habits in carrying out our work. When you have a habitual way of doing routine tasks, you don't need to think consciously about every detail. You can focus your conscious thinking on challenging problems and let the routine tasks fall into place naturally. Sometimes, the habits you develop slow the workflow. Because you don't consciously analyze your habits, you may not notice when this happens. Following are a couple of examples I notice frequently in my work with software development teams.

There's a tendency for people to struggle through problems on their own for some time before asking for help. It's not unusual for a team member to spend several days silently struggling with a problem. In most such cases, a second person could have cleared the mental logjam in a matter of seconds, if only the first person had asked for help. Replacing the habit of silent suffering with the habit of routine collaboration can have a significant positive effect on flow.

There's a tendency for people to assume they must get everything right on the first try. They spend considerable time reading, analyzing, and pondering before they ever dare lay hands on the keyboard. The truth is, you must get things right on the *last* try, not the first. When it comes to tool configuration or software design issues, it's almost always faster to find a solution through experimentation than it is to study the problem abstractly to the point that you'll solve it on the first attempt. Software isn't physical, so it's pretty cheap to throw it away and rewrite it in a different way.

4.5   *Summary*

In this chapter, you've seen how you can use metrics in combination to highlight opportunities for process improvement. You can combine process-related metrics, technical metrics, and human-factor metrics to obtain a clearer picture of the situation than you could hope to get by using a single metric in isolation.

The focus of process improvement is on maximizing throughput and on keeping the work flowing smoothly, without starts and stops or large variations in cycle time. Anything that causes delay, rework, or excessive accumulation of WIP inventory will reduce throughput and increase cycle time. You've also seen that irregular delivery, too much time spent on defect resolution, and stakeholder dissatisfaction can cause teams to disengage and stop caring about what they're doing. That has a detrimental effect on delivery performance and product quality.

Metrics can't tell you the exact root causes of delivery problems. Metrics can highlight time sinks where teams aren't adding customer-defined value to the product. This lets you know where to focus your root-cause analysis efforts to be sure you're addressing the right areas of the process. By examining the effect of WIP limits on a process, you've learned the good news that in most cases you can use a single lever to improve delivery performance: limiting WIP.

One final point about using metrics for process improvement as opposed to using them to track progress: the metrics you use to track progress remain in place throughout the project, whereas the metrics you use to inform process-improvement efforts are temporary. Once a tactical improvement goal has been achieved, you stop tracking the metrics you used to support that process improvement.

Planning predictability

5

This chapter covers

- The importance of predictability for short-term planning
- Using metrics to support predictable planning
- Common errors in the use of estimation for short-term planning
- Effects of high WIP levels on planning predictability

In this chapter, you'll see how metrics can support *planning predictability*. Predictable planning is critically important in software development and support regardless of the approach, process model, or delivery mode. When estimates and forecasts are informed by empirical data, they provide a more reliable indication of near-term future delivery performance than when they're based on individuals' subjective assessment.

In the early days of lightweight processes, people sometimes referred to traditional methods as *plan-based*, as distinct from *adaptive*. I think this is a misnomer, because all work is based on a plan, including adaptive development. The differences between traditional and adaptive methods have to do with when the planning is done and to what level of detail the plan must be elaborated before development work can begin.

For both approaches, it's important that actual progress align with expectations within some reasonable margin, a quality of planning known as *predictability*. When planning is predictable, you can be reasonably confident that you won't overshoot your not-to-exceed spending limit or miss a business opportunity by delivering too late. Lacking predictability, it becomes a matter of blind luck whether the outcome results in any value to stakeholders. Metrics can help both traditional and adaptive development approaches achieve greater predictability in planning.

5.1 Predictability and stakeholder satisfaction

One of the key benefits of tracking planning predictability is that it can enhance stakeholder satisfaction. In many organizations, delivery teams overcommit in an attempt to please stakeholders, and then they're unable to deliver as much as they promised. Stakeholders respond by demanding that the teams work faster. What they really want is predictability. The stakeholders need to be able to count on receiving whatever the teams claim they can deliver.

When stakeholders know they can count on receiving more or less what they're told to expect, they feel confident in the delivery organization and offer greater trust and autonomy to development teams. Whether delivery is faster isn't as important, provided expectations are set realistically. That confidence is usually repaid with smoother delivery and higher quality, because the teams don't need to use as much of their time preparing status reports and explaining why they failed to meet their commitments.

I'm not aware of any formal academic studies that correlate planning predictability with stakeholder satisfaction, but field experience suggests that they're strongly correlated. At several clients, I have tracked planning predictability and gauged stakeholder satisfaction through surveys or simple requests for them to self-rate their level of satisfaction on a 10-point scale. In all cases, stakeholder satisfaction was high when planning predictability was also high. When planning predictability was low, stakeholders tended to feel stressed and to lack trust in the development organization. They often responded by trying to control development directly. That generally leads to poorer delivery performance, which leads to lower trust, and so on. High planning predictability is to everyone's benefit.

5.1.1 Planning and traditional methods

With traditional development methods, planning occurs in large chunks. The basic approach entails a planning phase at the beginning of a project when risk-mitigation strategies are spelled out, requirements are elaborated in detail, dependencies are identified, work packages are defined, staffing levels are established, and fiduciary management plans are laid out. This is followed by a proportionally longer period of development during which teams execute the plan.

Lessons are always learned along the way, and the simplest pattern of planning and execution rarely plays out in reality. More often, the plan has to be adjusted or even significantly changed or re-baselined. This often requires changes in funding. The process to request additional funds may be cumbersome and time-consuming, and it may involve uncomfortable conversations about the reasons the original budget wasn't sufficient. This is largely due to the fact that traditional methods generally include long budget cycles and a big-budget-up-front approach to funding. Compounding the challenges, there's usually a belief that all design details, risks, and dependencies can be identified in advance, and that when this isn't the case it must be due to human error during the planning phase. To adjust funding after the initial budget has been allocated can require a major, top-down decision with significant political implications.

5.1.2   Planning and adaptive methods

With adaptive development methods, planning occurs throughout the delivery process. The general planning strategy is to identify risks early and otherwise defer decisions until close to the time when they must be made. You save the details about a feature until you're getting close to the time when you'll implement it. I've heard this approach called *rolling-wave planning, multiple planning horizons,* or *funnel planning.* There are probably many names for the same idea. One of the hallmarks of an adaptive approach is the use of an incremental funding model in which funds are kept liquid as long as possible so that they can be shifted (within limits) without requiring cumbersome procedures or the direct involvement of top management in every tactical decision.

A critical success factor for this approach is that the numerous short-term plans are reliable. Whether planning is based on forecasting, estimation, or something else, if delivery performance is unpredictable, then the plans will be unreliable. Metrics can help you understand whether actual delivery performance is reasonably consistent with expected delivery performance.

5.2   Measuring predictability

When stakeholders feel confident that they will receive what they were promised, life is better for everyone. Low predictability leads to stakeholder stress, stakeholder stress leads to micromanagement, micromanagement causes teams to feel they aren't being treated as professionals, and that feeling leads to disengagement and careless work. It's a vicious circle.

High predictability leads to trust; trust leads to autonomy for development teams, and autonomy leads to team member engagement, focus, and commitment. Metrics can help you understand how predictable your plans are and can point to potential improvements in predictability.

5.2.1   Estimation

Estimation is a process by which you try to get a sense of what is likely to happen in the future. You can use estimation to set expectations for delivery performance. When actual delivery performance is reasonably close to expectations, your plans are reliable. Otherwise, you can't predict how the work is likely to proceed, and you increase the risks of cost overruns and late delivery.

This isn't a book about estimation techniques, but it may be helpful to touch on a few general points to show how metrics can help you improve planning predictability. I'll start with a statement that may be provocative: estimates are informed guesses. People who make a living by using formal estimation methods don't like it when I say that, but when you're thinking about events that haven't yet occurred, an element of guesswork is involved. The ability to make an *informed* guess is a skill that can take years to master, and quite a few formal and informal methods have been devised to help you do it. Professional estimators prefer the word *know*, as in, "We need to know the cost up front." Of course, you can't know the future, in the plain sense of the English word. If you could, you wouldn't need to work for a living—you could predict which stocks to buy and where to live in order to avoid upcoming natural and man-made disasters. It's useful to keep in mind that your estimates are guesses, lest you forget that they're only approximations and come to depend on them too heavily for your own good. So, *guess* isn't a bad word; it's a healthy spoonful of sanity—a useful reminder of your natural limitations.

If estimates are informed guesses, then what, exactly, informs them? Generally, two types of input: information about past events, and peoples' subjective or gut-feel sense of what can be done. Through a combination of well-known statistical analysis techniques (amply described elsewhere) applied to historical data and an honest effort to avoid cognitive biases with respect to your interpretation of the data, you can arrive at reasonably good guesses about the future, provided you limit your predictions to a well-defined domain and a limited time frame.

Estimates that probe deeply into the future are valid at a high level of abstraction only. Estimates that deal with the near-term future can be more detailed. For example, you can't be confident about which task in a work breakdown structure (WBS) will be worked on on a given date two years from now, but you can be pretty confident about which tasks will be worked on next week.

One area of apparent confusion for IT practitioners is the fact that estimation is performed at different levels of detail for different purposes and at different times during a software development initiative. Debates among IT practitioners about estimation techniques tend to mix all kinds of estimation together, as if they were all the same. They aren't. It's perfectly okay to use different approaches to answer different kinds of questions.

The first critical decision to be made about a software development initiative is whether to do it at all. The drivers are different by domain: for-profit businesses need assurance that they will obtain a return on their investment; nonprofit organizations want to focus their limited resources on projects that promise to benefit the people they're chartered to help; and governments may have public service, political, or military objectives that supersede concerns about financial return. Estimates based on the way similar projects played out in the past can be useful to support a go/no-go decision about a proposed new project.

Once a development initiative is underway, the scope and nature of estimation change. At that stage, you're interested in steering the work toward a goal. For this sort of estimation, you can depend more on forecasting based on empirical observation of delivery performance. In some cases, it's feasible to dispense with estimation altogether and complete the work items in plan one by one. The right conditions have to be present to enable this approach; it's generally appropriate for small-scale initiatives involving a single, autonomous development team.

In all these cases, metrics can help you provide estimates that support planning predictability. For the purpose of this book, we're more interested in the latter case: steering the work once development has started.

5.2.2 *Forecasting*

Forecasting is an approach to estimation in which you set the expectation for near-term future performance by using recent past performance as a general indicator of how things are likely to proceed. It's an *empirical* (by observation) approach to estimation, rather than an analytical approach based on statistical methods.

When using a traditional approach, it's useful to compare observations of delivery of whatever artifacts are planned in each phase of development with the project plan. You saw this sort of measurement in chapter 2, when you compared the percentage of scope complete to date against the planned scope to date. Based on the observed rate of delivery, you can forecast the likely rate of delivery of the remaining deliverables in that phase. This can provide early warning of cost or schedule variance. I find cycle time the most practical metric to use for this purpose.

When using an adaptive approach with incremental delivery, you can forecast either the amount of time a team will need to complete a given scope or the amount of scope the team is likely to complete in a given time.

> **Pitfalls in estimation**
>
> I frequently observe four problems with the way people do estimation:
>
> - *Assuming that estimation means floating a guess as to how long it will take to complete a given piece of work*—Based on previous experience and quickly reasoning through the steps they expect to follow in completing the task, people toss out a number. This sort of gut-feel estimation may be necessary in the early stages of the work, before you have any observations of actual delivery performance on which to base forecasts; but when people rely on this method all the time, it can lead to a focus on improving the estimates rather than on delivering value.
> - *Performing bottom-up estimation*—People ask team members to estimate fine-grained tasks, and then they sum the estimates to arrive at an estimate for a whole release or even for the entire project. The natural estimation error

in each guess accumulates, rendering the final estimate all but meaningless. A top-down estimate based on historical delivery performance in projects of similar scope provides a better starting point.

- *Trying to achieve planning predictability by comparing estimated completion times with actual completion times*—This approach tends to encourage gaming the estimates to avoid punishment for incorrect guesses. Actual delivery remains out of sync with expectations, and the root causes aren't obvious because the gamed estimates hide the truth about what's happening.

- *Using estimates made by people other than those who carry out the work*—On some teams, a person in a technical leadership role estimates the tasks for the team. The individuals who will perform the work aren't consulted. Different individuals may require different amounts of time to complete similar tasks, and every individual requires a different amount of time than the person who made the estimates. Estimates arrived at in this manner are unlikely to be meaningful.

When no empirical data is available on which to base forecasts, you may have to rely on gut-feel guesses temporarily. You need to move away from guesswork and start to use more robust estimation methods as soon as you have enough observations to do so.

5.2.3 Predictability of traditional plans

Because traditional methods involve working for an extended time from a comprehensive plan, it's relatively easy to see whether the plan is predictable. You can use the same metrics you use to track general progress. When progress trends away from the plan, it indicates that the plan wasn't predictable.

Figure 5.1 repeats a figure from chapter 2 that shows the percentage of planned work packages that have been delivered as of the reporting date. A certain amount of variance may be expected, depending on the details of the project. When the variance exceeds that margin, it indicates that the project won't be completed as planned unless you take corrective action.

When this metric was introduced in chapter 2, the purpose was to track progress toward project goals. Here, you're using the same metric to gauge the predictability of the project plan. When stakeholders see that the work is on track, they'll feel confident in the team and allow them to work without interference. When stakeholders see that the plan is at risk, they'll tend to micromanage the work, which usually makes things worse. It's in everyone's interest to monitor the predictability of the plan and detect any problems as early as possible. In the best case, team members detect variance before stakeholders do and take corrective action on their own, to avoid the downward spiral of micromanagement.

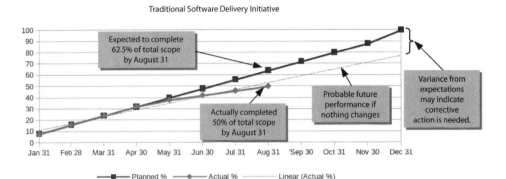

Figure 5.1   **Work packages complete to date compared to plan**

5.2.4   *Predictability of adaptive plans*

With adaptive development methods, planning occurs frequently throughout the project. Stakeholders monitor the results obtained in the smallest planning time frames to see how closely outcomes align with expectations. Depending on the process model and methodology in use, the smallest planning time frame might be called an *iteration*, a *sprint*, a *cadence*, or some other name, and it may represent a fixed or variable time period ranging from about one week to about three months. It's the time period for which development teams make their final refinement of the work queue or backlog prior to executing work items.

There are two general approaches to tracking planning predictability with adaptive methods. First, you can compare the amount of work you expected to deliver with the amount of work you actually delivered. Second, you can forecast short-term delivery performance based on empirical observation of recent past performance.

PERCENTAGE OF PLANNED WORK COMPLETED

Consider a team that uses a time-boxed iterative process model and measures delivery performance using velocity. If the team plans to complete 20 story points of work in a given iteration and actually delivers 18 story points of work, then they've delivered 90% of the planned work. If the organization regards, say, 15% variance to be normal, then this team's planning will be considered predictable.

Software developers are well known as optimists. When asked to estimate how long it will take them to complete a piece of work (or to size a user story in terms of points), they tend to underestimate. From quite a few years of work as a software developer, my observation is that there are a couple of reasons for this optimism. First, software developers tend to assume they won't encounter any unexpected obstacles in completing the work. They visualize the general path to success, and they feel ready to proceed.

Second, software developers enjoy a challenge and usually want to push the edge of the envelope in their own job performance.

You want to take the tendency toward optimism into account for purposes of short-term planning. If you know a development team consistently underestimates by a certain amount, then you can achieve predictable planning by adjusting your expectations accordingly. For example, consider a team that consistently predicts they will deliver 28 story points of work per iteration and that historically has delivered around 20 points per iteration. When they predict delivery of 28 points, you plan on receiving 20 points, and you set stakeholder expectations accordingly.

The metric is compelling because of its simplicity and because it feels comfortable to people who are accustomed to comparing estimates with actuals. It's widely used, because it's recommended by popular process frameworks that aim to extend agile methods to enterprise scale.

The chart in figure 5.2 shows a team's planning predictability over several iterations. On the surface this all seems reasonable enough, and I've seen it work as intended in one case. Due to that single positive example, I can't say categorically that it's always a bad idea. Let's just say it's *usually* a bad idea.

The pitfall lies with unintended motivational effects. As with any measurement that compares estimates with actuals, there's a risk that people will game the numbers to avoid negative performance appraisals. Furthermore, the basis of the calculation is velocity, a measure that is itself subject to gaming. Given a work environment where people feel it's risky to expose delivery problems, this metric is unlikely to provide

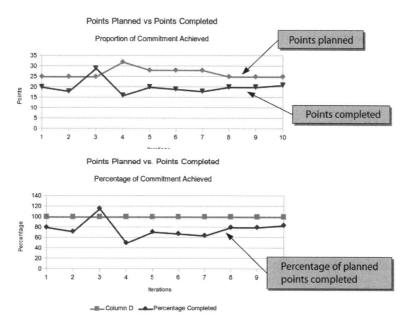

Figure 5.2   Proportion of commitment achieved

accurate information about planning predictability. Organizations often adopt this metric as part of a major restructuring and process change, which only exacerbates fears of negative consequences on the part of technical staff.

Another subtlety of human behavior comes into play whenever you express comparisons as percentages: people naturally want to see any percentage measurement come out as 100%. They will tend to game the numbers to cause their predictions to appear to be 100% correct. It isn't because people wish to cheat, but rather because they want positive things to be 100% positive.

Normally, teams do one or both of two things: they game their story sizes so that they'll achieve the number of story points they wish to see, or they adjust their commitments based on recent short-term variations in their performance. In this example, in the wake of an unusually productive iteration 3, the team confidently assumed they could continue the upward trend. When iteration 4 came in below expectations, they adjusted their plans for iteration 5 downward. These were merely reactions to single data points, not predictable planning.

I generally recommend that teams use empirically based forecasting to ensure predictable planning, rather than track percentage of commitment achieved or rely on subjective estimation. It's possible you'll be required to use a comparative metric in your organization, so you need to understand how it works. Just be aware of the potential motivational effects, and be prepared to deal with them.

FORECASTING

Forecasting avoids the behavioral problems inherent in comparing estimates with actuals. With forecasting, you don't depend on estimates. You observe the team's past performance and extend it into the future. It makes no difference whether team members are optimistic or fearful or hungry for a challenge or anything else. All that matters is their actual delivery performance in the recent past.

Success factors are as follows:

- Consider recent performance in the past three or four contiguous iterations. Don't go back too far into the past, because every team's performance changes over time.

- Limit future projections to the short term. The further into the future you look, the less accurate your forecasts will be.

- Take into account temporary variations in the team's delivery capacity, such as planned company events, planned vacations, and so forth.

This approach is sometimes called *yesterday's weather.* The idea is that today's weather is likely to be similar to yesterday's weather.

Forecasts can be based on any reliable, empirical measure of delivery performance. In practice, this boils down to two metrics: velocity and cycle time. Velocity can be used with a time-boxed iterative process. Cycle time can be used with any process.

FORECASTING BASED ON VELOCITY

When a time-boxed iterative process model is used properly and velocity isn't gamed, velocity provides an empirical measure of the team's delivery capacity. You can use velocity from recent iterations to forecast the likely velocity in the next iteration or two.

To understand how forecasting provides better predictability than comparing estimates with actuals, let's consider a team that's using a time-boxed iterative process model and needs to plan the approximate amount of work they will be able to deliver in the upcoming iteration. In the spreadsheet accompanying the book, the data is shown in the sheet named Velocity for Forecasting.

In this scenario, the team plans their work for the next iteration by making a commitment to deliver some amount of work. They're keen to improve their performance, so they set an optimistic target as inspiration. In addition, stakeholders are interested in receiving as much software as possible in each iteration. Time after time, the team plans to deliver more results than is realistic based on their performance to date. Stakeholders continue to ask for more, because they want to make up for lost time. The team agrees to deliver more, because they want to catch up. Yet however earnestly the interested parties wish for more, the team can only deliver what it can deliver.

Figure 5.3 shows how the scenario might play out over the course of 12 iterations. The team repeatedly commits to delivering 30 story points of work per iteration, despite never having done so. They feel as if they're close to the mark and that if they just try a little harder next time, they're sure to reach the goal. From the stakeholders' perspective, the team doesn't appear to be trying to do better—it only appears that

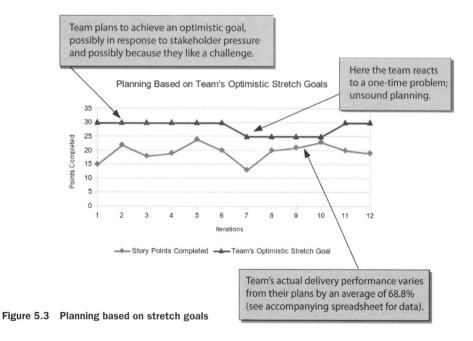

Figure 5.3   Planning based on stretch goals

they over-promise and under-deliver. The stakeholders increase delivery pressure on the team in hopes they can speed up. The team assures the stakeholders that they can, indeed, speed up. The stakeholders are dissatisfied.

Notice that there's a fairly high degree of subjectivity in these plans. When the team experiences a better-than-average iteration, they take it as a sign that they're on the verge of a performance breakthrough, and they plan accordingly. When they experience a below-average iteration, they assume it represents a downward change in their delivery capacity, and they reduce their stretch goal accordingly. This sort of vacillation reduces planning predictability.

In this example, the team's short-term planning predictability is 68.8%. If you assume the organization regards variance of 85% to be acceptable, then this team isn't performing at an acceptable level.

Forecasting differs from this approach in that no one asks how much work the team believes or wishes it can deliver. They look only at the team's demonstrated delivery performance. Let's examine the same 12 iterations by the same team and see how their planning predictability would play out if they used yesterday's weather to forecast delivery performance; see figure 5.4.

In this scenario, the team lets the chips fall where they may in the first couple of iterations. They could have floated a guess as to how many story points they could deliver; but ultimately it would make no difference, because beginning with iteration 4, they use a calculated value as their forecast. They use a sliding window of three iterations to calculate their likely delivery performance in the next iteration.

In the spreadsheet, you can see that this approach results in planning predictability of 89.9%. This is within the organization's acceptable variance, so the team is deemed to be performing well. Yet the performance is exactly the same as in the previous example. The only difference is in the expectations the team sets with stakeholders.

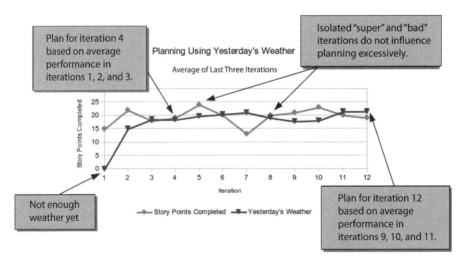

Figure 5.4 Planning using yesterday's weather

Forecasting based on empirical observation of the team's performance sets more realistic expectations than stretch goals or subjective estimation methods.

FORECASTING BASED ON CYCLE TIME

When I introduced cycle time in chapter 2, I mentioned that it's useful for predictable planning. It provides an empirical measure of a team's delivery performance. Cycle time (CT) is more flexible than velocity for this purpose, because it has no dependencies on the process model or delivery mode used.

Although CT doesn't require a time-boxed iterative process model, it's useful to define a fixed time period for collecting observations. Continuous-flow process frameworks typically recommend fixed-length *cadences* for development work and for releases. When you know your mean CT per month or per week or per iteration, then you can use it to forecast your likely delivery performance in the next month, week, or iteration.

For the purpose of predictability, the key factor you're interested in is the variation in CT within one standard deviation of the mean. You typically ignore outliers beyond this range for the purpose of short-term planning. Variation within this range is considered *common-cause* variation—that is, variation due to the *system* in which the work takes place. In a software development and delivery process, the system comprises organizational structure, standard procedures, process steps, and so forth. As long as these factors don't change much, your team's delivery performance will remain consistent. Variation beyond one standard deviation of the mean is usually caused by one-time issues; it's called *special-cause* variation. You don't want to include special-cause variation in your forecast, because it's unpredictable and unlikely to recur.

Figure 5.5 shows a CT plot for a team that has significant variation in CT for its tasks. Keep in mind the difference between *accuracy* and *precision*. Because CT is empirical, it will be accurate. But it can only be as precise as the variation allows. With high variation, you have accuracy but not precision. Your confidence in the forecast is high within the 1 SD range. In this example, that's between about 5.5 and 38.5 hours per task—a pretty wide range. High variability correlates with low predictability. The longer the cadence, the less precise the forecast will be. If you're working on a one-month development cadence, your planning predictability will be lower than with a two-week cadence.

To improve flow as well as predictability, the team can reexamine its work practices and management can reexamine organizational structure and standard procedures. Let's say your organization takes some of those steps. Regarding organizational structure, perhaps you align some of the value-producing teams and assets more closely with the value stream and adjust team composition to include all necessary skills, reducing the number of dependencies on groups outside the team to get tasks done. Regarding process, perhaps you fold some of the governance reviews into the development process so that they no longer require a separate approval step. Regarding development practices, perhaps you soften the boundaries between specialists on the team and encourage greater collaboration, reducing the number of hand-offs and

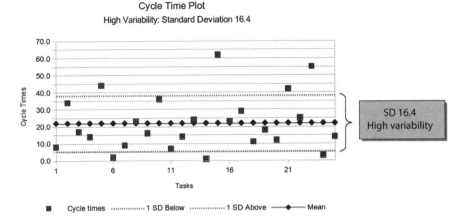

Figure 5.5 **Percentage of planned work completed. The mean CT is 22 hours, but high variability means you have low confidence in a forecast based on mean CT. CT varies between 1 and 62 hours. Within 1 SD, the range is between 5.6 and 38.5 hours. A forecast based on 22 hours will be accurate within a range of about 32.8 hours. That's highly accurate but not precise. The longer the cadence or iteration length, the greater the effect of variation on planning predictability.**

back-flows, and you adopt technical practices that build in quality from the outset, reducing back-flows for defect correction.

These improvements could have an impact on CT and on planning predictability, as shown in figure 5.6. Now mean CT is 16.6 hours, with common-cause variation of about 13.1 hours. This represents a substantial improvement. You've shortened the mean CT and reduced variation considerably. There's still variation, and there always

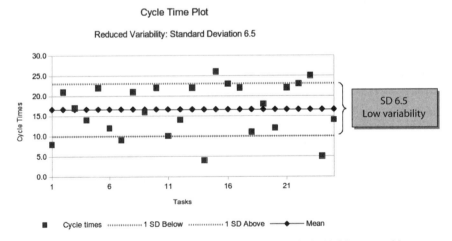

Figure 5.6 **Percentage of planned work completed. The mean CT is 16.6 hours, and low variability means you can have moderately high confidence in a forecast based on mean CT. CT varies between 4 and 26 hours. Within 1 SD, the range is between 10.1 and 23.2 hours. A forecast based on 16.6 hours will be precise within a range of about 13.1 hours.**

will be. Software development isn't a repeatable, assembly-line process; it's a creative process, and variation is only to be expected. Even so, by reducing the variation, you've improved planning predictability.

5.3 *Predictability in unpredictable workflows*

In the section on velocity in chapter 2, one of the anti-patterns pertains to teams that have a mixed workflow consisting of some planned work and some unplanned work, such as production support. This sort of mixed workflow is inherently less predictable than workflows consisting purely of planned work or purely of ongoing support. Tracking appropriate metrics can help you improve predictability in short-term planning for teams that have a mixed workflow.

Teams that use a time-boxed iterative process model often deal with mixed workflows by setting aside a percentage of their available time to handle any unplanned work that may come their way mid-iteration. The challenge is in deciding how much time to set aside. If they guess too low, they'll fail to complete their planned work. If they guess too high, they'll have idle time with no work ready to start. Fortunately, you can track a couple of simple measurements to deal with this situation:

- Mean CT, tracked separately for planned and unplanned work
- The average number of unplanned work items that enter the team's workflow in the middle of an iteration (with a time-boxed iterative process) or development cadence (with a continuous-flow process)

Once you have at least three iterations' or cadences' worth of observations, you can forecast the approximate amount of time the team needs to set aside for unplanned work in the near-term future. For example, consider the following data points:

- Mean CT for planned work items: 10 hours
- Mean CT for unplanned work items: 16 hours
- Average number of unplanned work items per iteration: 4
- Time available for value-add work based on team member availability:
  24 hours × 6 team members = 144 hours

Given 4 unplanned work items on average, with completion time averaging 16 hours, the team needs to set aside about 64 hours per iteration for unplanned work. That leaves 144 − 64 = 80 hours available for planned work. With a mean CT of 10 hours for planned work items, the team can take on about 8 items from the planned work queue or product backlog per iteration.

Because this forecast is based on empirical observation of actual performance in the recent past, it will be more accurate regarding near-term future performance than estimation or commitment-based plans. I suggest using a sliding window of three to five iterations or cadences as the basis for forecasting.

In addition to improving planning predictability, these metrics will provide information to support process-improvement goals. If 80 productive hours per iteration doesn't align with organizational performance goals, then you know (and can demonstrate to management) that changes are needed. You may *feel* as if the unplanned work is interfering with your ability to support business objectives, but that may not be sufficient to gain the support of management. Having real data to support your case gives you a better chance of gaining support for an improvement initiative.

5.4 *Effects of high variation in work item sizes*

Software development teams package their planned work in units that have different names and different scopes depending on the methods they use. A work item may be called a *requirement*, a *work package*, a *user story*, a *minimum marketable feature*, a *use case*, or something else.

Each term has a specific definition according to one or another software development methodology, but all the definitions have something in common: they represent a chunk of software functionality that is *usable* by someone to achieve some goal. Any of those work items, when completed, could potentially be sold to the public or included in a production deployment of the application.

5.4.1 *Deployable units of work*

Let's say you're building a banking application to manage customer accounts. The feature to transfer funds from one account to another isn't usable by a customer if it can remove the funds from account A but not put the funds into account B. The software has to perform both of those operations in order to be useful. Similarly, a customer can't use an online store application that can collect selected items in a shopping cart but can't process the sale transaction. I doubt you would wish to use a word processor that could display what you type but not save the document, or pilot a spacecraft whose flight-control software could start the rocket motor but not stop it. Those examples represent *parts* of software features, not complete features.

It's only natural, then, for people to define work items that correspond with useful functionality. The kinds of work items defined in various software development methodologies generally represent meaningful, useful features. A *use case* describes all the interactions between an actor and a system that occur during some meaningful activity. A *user story* describes an interaction between a user and a system that provides some sort of value to the user. A *minimum marketable feature* includes enough functionality that a customer would be willing to pay real money for it. A *work package*, designed for traditional linear methods, includes enough valuable functionality to make it worth the cost of pushing it through a lengthy process of review, testing, and governance.

5.4.2 Trackable units of work

The challenge for predictable planning lies in the fact that these work items may vary significantly in size (effort or time). In a banking system, it may be trivial to build code to display a list of the customer's active accounts, somewhat more complicated to complete the funds-transfer feature, and even more complicated to build the code to determine the customer's eligibility for special offers. The code to switch a rocket motor on and off might be simple, whereas the code to keep the craft stable during reentry could be extremely complicated. If you forecast performance based on the observed cycle times for work items like those, you'll have high variability and low predictability.

The variation in sizes makes it difficult to achieve planning predictability. The solution is to distinguish between the work items you define for purposes of planning and tracking, and the units of functionality you can deliver to production or to the market. You can decompose large features into workable pieces that are all more or less the same size in order to minimize CT variation and improve planning predictability. Those workable, trackable pieces of work need not be individually deployable or marketable.

The work items must have a clear definition of *done*, for purposes of measuring CT. That may take whatever form makes sense in context: perhaps the software passes automated tests, or passes a technical review, or can be demonstrated to key stakeholders who accept it. Provided the work items are roughly the same size and there's a practical way to determine when they're finished, you can use mean CT to achieve accurate forecasting and predictable planning.

5.4.3 Demonstrating the value of consistently sized work items

When combined with other metrics, CT can provide strong hints about potential process improvements. Let's consider a team that's using a time-boxed iterative process. The team represents requirements as user stories and estimates the stories using relative sizing in terms of story points.

It's common for teams that work this way to have user stories that vary significantly in relative size. It can be challenging to help team members understand the value of learning to craft user stories that are roughly the same size. Teams tend to focus on completing story points in order to receive credit toward velocity. They may not see variation in user-story size as an important factor for effective delivery.

By juxtaposing CT observations with estimated user-story sizes, you can show a correlation between small, consistent story size and stable CTs. When such effects are made visible, teams tend to work toward improving the numbers.

You already know that high variability in CTs correlates with low planning predictability. When you juxtapose trends in estimated user-story sizes with trends in CT, you can see that there's a direct correlation. Therefore, high variability in estimated story sizes correlates with low planning predictability. In the example in figure 5.7, the team delivers 20 stories totaling 300 story points. The stories are spread across several iterations. At any given point in the delivery process, it's hard for the team to predict how many stories they'll deliver in the next iteration.

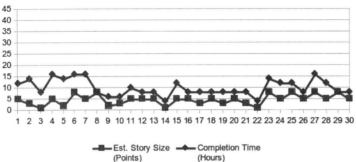

Figure 5.7   You can't compare points with hours, but you can observe that trends follow the same pattern: high variability in estimated story sizes correlates with high variability in CTs and with low planning predictability.

When the team splits stories so they're closer to the same size, CT variability is reduced and planning predictability is improved (see figure 5.8). The team delivers about the same number of story points, but the points are spread across 30 user stories instead of 20, and the story sizes are more consistent. At any time, the team can predict the number of user stories they're likely to deliver in the next iteration.

When you correlate CT with user-story sizes, you're using metrics to support process improvement rather than tracking delivery progress. Delivery performance will improve as a result of adopting more effective practices.

In the context of traditional methods, this means decomposing work packages into similarly sized tasks and keeping the general size of these tasks fairly small. In the context of adaptive methods, this means writing, splitting, and sizing user stories (or similar artifacts by whatever name). The goal is to help the team learn to craft user

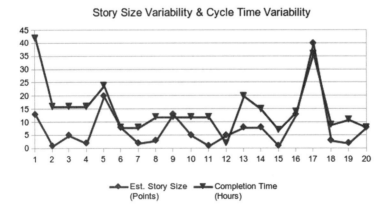

Figure 5.8   By splitting stories to reduce the range of sizes, you reduce CT variability and improve planning predictability.

stories that represent vertical slices of functionality and to minimize the range of user-story sizes.

These practices help teams deliver business value more smoothly and steadily. In turn, smooth delivery improves planning predictability, which is correlated with stakeholder satisfaction.

5.5 Effects of high work-in-process levels

It's generally known that when you try to juggle too many tasks, it takes you longer to complete them all than it would if you tackled one or two of them at a time. Yet many software development teams try to work on many items concurrently. By juxtaposing WIP levels with other metrics, you can help teams, management, and business stakeholders understand the value of limiting WIP and focusing on getting a few things done at a time.

5.5.1 Work in process, cycle time, process cycle efficiency, and throughput

In some cases, business stakeholders or senior management have the misconception that by *starting* many tasks, teams are *making progress* on all of them. Many technical professionals make the same assumption. This misconception has been fed and nurtured for decades, thanks to a persistent focus in management training on maximizing resource utilization, as well as the fear on the part of technical personnel that they'll lose their jobs unless they appear to be busy at all times.

All the work that's been officially started but not yet finished is called *work in process* (WIP). According to the Lean school of thought, WIP is a form of *inventory*, and inventory is a form of *waste*. If you're genuinely interested in maximizing the value you deliver to stakeholders, then you need to find the level of WIP that yields the highest throughput, given the details of your process.

Before you can correct the problem, you have to teach others in the organization that WIP is an issue in the first place. To do *that*, you need numbers. You can show the effect of excessive WIP on delivery performance by correlating CT with WIP. Shorter CT means higher throughput.

Let's consider a contrived example to illustrate the point. The following figures depict a work queue containing five work items and show where time is spent as the team completes the items. Real-world situations follow the same pattern on a larger scale and with numerous distracting details, so I'm intentionally using a simplified example to show the effect.

In the first scenario (see figure 5.9), the team pulls all five items into the *in progress* state at the same time. Let's walk through this scenario and see what's going on.

At hour 0, the team begins a period of work. For a traditional project, this could be a phase in a linear process model, such as requirements elaboration or code construction. The work items in that case would consist of the tasks required to complete specific artifacts, such as requirements specifications ready to be coded or units of

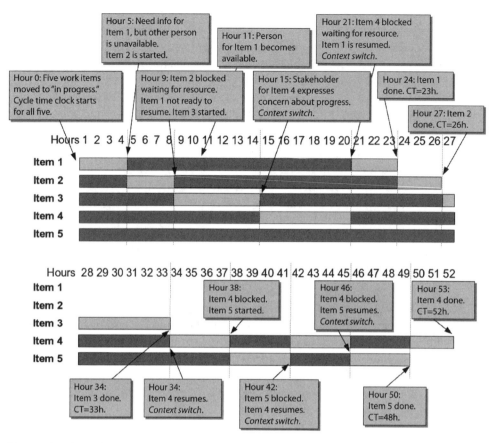

Figure 5.9   Effect of high WIP on CT: scenario 1

code ready to be tested. For an adaptive project, it could be the length of a time-boxed iteration or a development cadence. The work items might represent vertical slices of functionality to be finished to the point that they're production ready. For a hybrid process, the work items might represent chunks of work somewhere between a task and a vertical slice of functionality. The general effects of high WIP are the same in all cases; there's no dependency on development approach, process model, or delivery mode.

In this scenario, the team pulls all the work scheduled for the new work period into the in-progress status at the same time. The CT clock starts at hour 0 for all five work items. But it isn't possible to work on five things at the same time. Notwithstanding the fact that all five items are officially in progress, only one at a time receives direct attention at any given moment. (This is a bit of a simplification, because most teams have enough resources to work on more than one item at a time. This fact doesn't invalidate the model.)

The team works on item 1 until they reach an impasse. In the meantime, items 2, 3, 4, and 5 are in a wait state. They're officially in progress, so they count as WIP. They're a contrasting shade in figure 5.9 to show that no value is being added to them during the first four hours.

The team's immediate response to hitting a block on item 1 is to turn their attention to item 2. This is one of the insidious ways that high WIP contributes to long CTs—because another work item is ready for action, the team makes no special effort to resolve the blocker on item 1. People tend to focus on whatever demands their attention. Therefore, the people who can help the team resolve the blocker tend to wait until the team asks them to do something. Until then, they help others who *do* ask them.

The team repeats the same behavior when they hit blocks in hour 9 and hour 15. Now they have four work items partially complete and nothing finished. The person they need to help them get item 1 moving again was available as of hour 11, but the team was busy doing something else in hour 11. They didn't get back to item 1 until hour 21.

Once they did so, they finished item 1 in just three hours. But they also experienced a *context-switch event*, which incurs a cost in time. Every time a person switches contexts, it takes a few minutes for them to get back to the point where they left off when they set the task aside. Different studies have found different costs for context switching, ranging from about 10 minutes to about two hours per event. Context-switching overhead associated with juggling many active tasks causes CTs to stretch out. For purposes of this example, I'm assuming that each context-switch event costs 30 minutes.

The team continues to work in the same manner until all five work items have been completed. Total time: 52 hours. Here are the CT observations:

- Item 1: 23 hours
- Item 2: 26 hours
- Item 3: 33 hours
- Item 4: 49 hours
- Item 5: 52 hours
- Mean CT: 36.6 hours
- Process cycle efficiency (PCE): 28.2%
- Throughput, hours 0–20: 0 items
- Throughput, hours 21–40: 3 items

Let's see what might be different if the team minimizes WIP, as illustrated in figure 5.10. At the outset, the team pulls only one work item into in-progress status. The CT clock starts for item 1. They work on this item until they hit a blocker. Because the team is focusing on just one work item, they immediately try to remove the blocker. In the hypothetical scenario, they're unable to remove the blocker, and they need to wait for someone to become available to help them with it. Having done what they can for now on item 1, the team pulls item 2 into in-progress status, starting its CT clock.

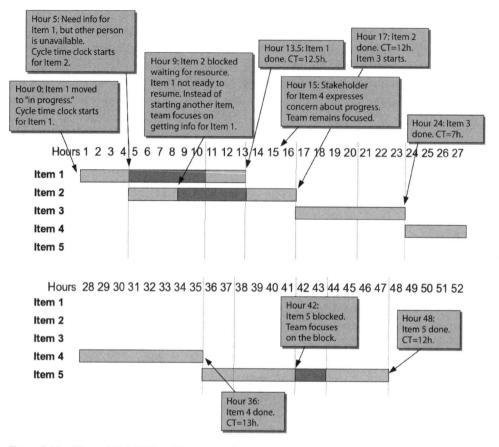

Figure 5.10   Effect of high WIP on CT: scenario 2

Hour 9: The team hits a blocker on item 2. This time, because they're intentionally keeping WIP to a minimum, they turn their attention to removing the blockers on items 1 and 2. They don't start item 3, even though this means they appear to be idle. They aren't idle at all; they're trying to get the first two work items moving again, which is the most valuable thing they can do at this point.

Hour 11: The blocker on item 1 is removed, and the team completes that item.

Hour 13: The blocker on item 2 is removed, and the team completes that item.

Hour 15: The stakeholder for item 4 expresses concern about progress on his work, just as occurred in the first scenario. This time, however, the team doesn't drop whatever they're doing to try and satisfy that stakeholder. Instead, they stick to their plan and continue working on item 3. Doing so serves the interest of the stakeholder for item 4, whether he understands that or not. This is clear when you note that in the first scenario, item 4 was completed at hour 53, with a CT of 52 hours; in the second scenario, it's completed in hour 36, with a CT of 13 hours—significantly better delivery performance.

Hour 17: Item 2 is completed with a CT of 12 hours.

Hour 24: Item 3 is completed with a CT of 7 hours.

Hour 36: Item 4 is completed with a CT of 13 hours.

In the first scenario, item 5 was blocked at hour 42 for four hours. In the second scenario, the same block occurs at the same point, but this time the team is focused on getting item 5 done. They aren't distracted by context switching to a different task, and they're able to resolve the blocker in half the time. On the whole, by eliminating context-switch events and pushing a rapid solution to the blocker, the team saved six hours on item 5.

Here are the numbers for the second scenario:

- Item 1: 12.5 hours
- Item 2: 12 hours
- Item 3: 7 hours
- Item 4: 13 hours
- Item 5: 12 hours
- Mean CT: 11.3 hours
- PCE: 78.2%
- Throughput, hours 0–20: 2 items
- Throughput, hours 21–40: 2 items

So, what do these numbers tell you?

- The team's CT is consistent. Except for item 3, they completed any given work item in about the same amount of time—roughly 12 hours. This wasn't visible in scenario 1, because by pulling *all* the work items into in-progress status at the same time, the team was hiding information about what was really happening in their process. They made their process *opaque* and therefore difficult to measure or improve.

- Throughput is more consistent in scenario 2 than in scenario 1. The effects of high WIP in scenario 1 tended to pile up incomplete work, which was eventually finished near the end of the delivery process. With scenario 2, you can see that the team generally delivers about two work items every 20 hours. This supports the goal of predictable planning.

- The fate of item 4 is informative. In scenario 1, item 4 hit a blocker at hour 38 and another at hour 46. In scenario 2, these organizational events had no effect on item 4, because item 4 was completed at hour 36. This illustrates one of the insidious effects of high WIP: the longer a work item remains in active status, the greater the chance that an organizational issue will arise that blocks progress. The phrase *organizational issue* sounds pretty serious, but it needn't be anything more unusual than a person being busy with other work at the time when your team needs their help. When you go ahead and get things finished, nothing can block them.

- In scenario 1, the team lost considerable time to context-switching overhead and to delayed resolution of blockers as a direct result of high WIP. Their PCE was much higher in scenario 2; that is, the team spent proportionally more of the available time doing value-add work and proportionally less time waiting.

When context switching is good

As a general rule, context switching causes delay and error because it breaks people's train of thought. But a general rule isn't a universal truth. In knowledge work, people sometimes reach a mental impasse. They can't think of what to do next. They can't see the cause of a simple problem. As the expression goes, they can't see the forest for the trees.

When that happens, it's often useful to take a break from the task at hand. You can stand up and stretch, take a walk, talk about last night's game—anything to clear your mind. You might even set the task aside and work on a different task for a while.

The point of this section is not to suggest that you avoid context switching at all costs. The point is to help you understand the impact of excessive context switching on throughput and CT. When you make a trade-off, be aware of what you're trading for what. Trade a context switch for clarity of mind when you need it. Don't trade high WIP for high throughput.

5.5.2 *Work in process and defect density*

Defect density is usually shown as the number of reported software defects per 1,000 lines of source code (KLOC). When you think about software defects from a Lean point of view, you realize that any effort expended to detect, track down, and fix defects is *waste*, according to Lean's definition; that is, it's activity that doesn't add value to the product.

You could argue that removing defects makes the product better and therefore increases its value, but Lean thinking has a narrower definition of *value* than that. Customers aren't interested in paying for bug fixes; they're only interested in paying for properly working features. In that sense, defect correction doesn't add any customer-defined value to the product. As far as customers are concerned, the product should have been correct the first time.

Defects may be introduced in a software product for a variety of reasons. One of the potential causes is that the team is juggling too many tasks simultaneously. People can lose focus, overlook details, and neglect loose ends when they frequently context-switch across multiple tasks. They introduce defects they wouldn't have introduced, had they been able to focus on one or two tasks at a time. Then, when they go back to address the defects, the defect-correction activity becomes yet another task to be juggled along with all the other things they're working on. At the same time, more and more changes have to be integrated into the code base, and each merge increases the risk of introducing another defect. The problem snowballs.

Thanks to the longstanding and widespread misconception that it's more effective to start many tasks than it is to concentrate on completing one task at a time, people who have slipped into this pattern may not be able to see a way out. You can use metrics to help them see how high WIP tends to increase defect density. It's easy to pull WIP levels from a Kanban board, a task board, or any electronic project-management tool. If you're tracking defect density, or even just counting reported bugs, you can correlate these two pieces of information. It will become obvious that they change in direct proportion to one another.

What accounts for this correlation? In my experience, it comes down to the cause-and-effect pattern shown in figure 5.11's diagram of effects.

High WIP tends to have two immediate effects: increased context-switching overhead and overutilization of team members. You've seen how high WIP leads to increased context switching as people try to juggle many tasks simultaneously. You've also seen that this results in longer CTs.

High WIP also leads to overutilization, the enemy of throughput. With many tasks in play, teams tend to spread team members across as many tasks as they can, hoping to keep more of them in an active state and fewer of them in a waiting state at any given time. It's not uncommon for teams to have more than twice as many work items in an in-progress state as they have team members. Everyone is juggling two or more work items.

This makes collaboration all but impossible. Individual team members work by themselves and don't enjoy the benefits of paired work or group work. They must struggle alone through each problem that comes up; they lack a second pair of eyes with which to see the forest for the trees. When another team member *could* help resolve a problem, chances are that person is unavailable because they're also juggling multiple tasks. Without the opportunity for direct collaboration within and across functional specialties, different kinds of interim artifacts have to be handed off through formal process steps such as reviews and quality gates, and indirect communication media such as documents. All these factors add to CT as well as increasing the probability of miscommunication, which often results in defects.

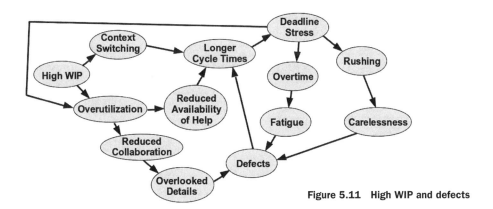

Figure 5.11 High WIP and defects

Increased CTs tend to result in three undesirable behaviors: overtime, rushing, and overutilization. When people begin to worry about meeting deadlines or delivery commitments, there's a tendency to work longer hours to try to make up for lost time. People may also cut corners and rush through tasks in an attempt to finish their work faster. Programmers may decide to dispense with refactoring as they modify the code base, resulting in technical debt that increases CT insidiously in the long term. Software testers may skip test cases in an attempt to complete the testing work more quickly. Analysts may gloss over details in an attempt to prepare requirements faster.

These behaviors generally lead to more defects, creating a vicious circle, more properly called a *reinforcing loop*. You can follow the arrows in figure 5.11 to locate the reinforcing loops it depicts.

Stress over deadlines often leads to a third undesirable behavior: overutilization. You can see that this forms another reinforcing loop. Even if the team didn't begin its work with team members overutilized, the emotional response to deadline pressure often causes teams to throw people at the problem. They may be tempted to set aside robust collaboration practices such as pair programming in the belief that allocating individuals to more tasks will speed things up. They may pull even more work items into in-progress, hoping that by designating the work items as active, progress will somehow be made on them. How many times have you heard managers ask, "How many more people do you need to meet the deadline?" There may be cases when a team doesn't have enough people to handle its workload, but more often than not, throwing people at the problem only makes matters worse.

The root cause of most of this is high WIP, and the simplest remedy is to limit WIP. All this may appear obvious to you. Unfortunately, it isn't obvious to everyone. I've found that by showing people the correlation between high WIP and defects, you can open a dialogue with team members and project stakeholders to bring the workflow under control and improve delivery performance.

5.6   Summary

In this chapter, you saw how metrics can help you improve the predictability of your short-term planning. Predictable short-term planning helps keep work on track, enhances stakeholder satisfaction, and builds trust in the organization. The proper choice of metrics for estimation and forecasting improves planning predictability, whereas poor choices reduce predictability. Common misconceptions about development methods, work-item definitions, estimation techniques, and metrics can give you false readings of progress and lead to unpredictable planning. High variability in work-item size and high work-in-process levels can cause performance variance and hide information about progress.

Reporting outward and upward

At higher levels of management, people make different kinds of decisions than would be made at the team level. They need to know what's going on across an entire program, an entire product suite, an entire value stream, or the entire enterprise. Whereas you make decisions about how to keep the work moving forward, they make decisions about whether a project should be continued or canceled, and whether a given initiative ought to be capitalized or expensed. Details about individual work packages or user stories aren't helpful for that kind of decision-making. Those individuals need relevant, summarized information without any clutter.

At the same time, software development teams must be able to focus on their work without being distracted by administrative activities such as recording the number of hours they worked or estimating the expected completion date for a given software feature. Distractions like those interrupt flow, create delay, increase lead times, raise costs, and cause stress.

In this chapter, you'll see how to provide measurements that are useful to upper management without expending excessive effort in doing so. You'll also explore some of the issues that can arise when management expectations for upward reporting conflict with the metrics you've chosen to help you steer your work at the team level. You'll also see how you, as the person responsible for reporting metrics, can collect the data you need without interfering with your teams' day-to-day work.

I suggest that one of your functions is to act as an insulating layer between your teams and the organization. What does this mean? Others in the organization need to collect information from teams. Yet every interruption and every administrative task reduces the teams' effectiveness. As a person responsible for tracking progress, you can help teams maximize their effectiveness by handling administrative requirements on their behalf.

6.1   *Reporting hours*

Few issues cause more grumbling on technical teams than the requirement that people track the number of hours they spend working on each project. Contemporary wisdom in software development is to dedicate each team to a single project at a time. Even then, team members don't enjoy taking time to track the hours they spend on project work compared with the hours they spend on other tasks. In traditional organizations, teams may work on multiple projects concurrently, and in many organizations individuals may be allocated to multiple teams and multiple projects in a complicated matrix structure. Tracking the hours spent on each project each day can become a time-consuming activity whose value isn't obvious to technical workers.

Management needs to know where the time is spent for capitalized projects. Capitalization provides a tax benefit by allowing companies to spread the initial development cost of a software solution over the anticipated production lifetime of the solution. Management has to track costs closely. All the costs except labor are pretty straightforward to track, because they're mostly fixed costs. To get the labor cost, management depends on staff to report the hours they spend working on each capitalized project.

This is probably uninteresting to you, and it's definitely uninteresting to your teams, because your focus is execution, not funding. Knowing how each team member spends each hour doesn't help you execute the project. Spending time tracking hours certainly doesn't help team members complete any work. It isn't a value-add activity; it's administrative overhead. Pursuant to your function as an insulating layer, you need to provide this information to management without asking anything of your team members.

But if you don't ask them, how will you know how team members spend their time? The answer is clear, if you remember that you want to provide decision-makers with information *at the right level of detail*. Management doesn't need to know exactly how Mary Smith spent every minute of every day. They need to know that Mary's team spent more or less the expected amount of time working on capitalized project A and on capitalized project B.

6.1.1 An example

Let's say that over the span of projects A and B, the team is expected to spend about half their time working on each. Management needs to know whether that expectation was met. They don't need to know that in week 1 the team split their time 70/30 between the two, and in week 2 they split their time 30/70. That level of detail doesn't help management make the decisions they're responsible for making. They certainly don't need to know all the minor variations of each individual team member's time; they only need aggregate numbers.

To report accurate information about hours at the right level of detail, you can depend on some basic assumptions. First, you can assume that variations in time allocation will wash out over the course of a project. Approximate data will be accurate and useful to support management decision-making. Second, you can assume that most individuals will work a standard week unless something unusual happens. You needn't ask people to report their hours in painstaking detail—you only need to know about variances from the standard work week. Figure 6.1 shows an example of how this can work.

The spreadsheet tracks the total work hours put in by each of 10 team members on a team that's working on four projects. The team is allocated 40% to project A, 30% to project B, 20% to project C, and 10% to project D. Most of the time, team members work a 40-hour work week. You don't need to ask them how many hours they work in a normal week—it's standard. When they're on vacation, it's on the team calendar, and you don't need to ask them. When they're out of the office, they let you know by

A	B	C	D	E	F	G	H	I	J	K	L
	Mary	Venkat	Furniko	Luc	Alice	Chin	Dennis	Guadalupe	Rosario	Ken	
1	40	40	40	20	40	0	40	32	40	40	
2	40	30	40	20	40	0	40	42	40	40	
3	40	40	40	40	40	44	40	40	40	40	
4	40	40	40	40	40	40	40	40	40	40	
5	32	40	40	40	40	40	40	40	40	40	
6	40	40	40	40	40	40	40	40	20	40	
7	40	40	40	40	40	40	40	40	32	40	
8	40	32	40	40	40	40	40	40	40	40	
9	40	32	40	40	40	40	48	40	40	30	
10	24	40	40	40	16	40	40	40	40	40	
11	40	40	40	40	0	40	36	40	40	40	
12	40	40	40	40	24	40	40	40	0	40	
13	40	40	40	40	40	40	40	40	0	40	
14	40	40	40	40	40	40	0	40	40	20	
15	40	40	40	40	40	40	0	40	40	40	
16	32	28	40	40	40	40	40	40	40	40	
17	40	40	48	40	40	40	40	40	40	40	
18	40	40	32	40	40	40	40	40	40	40	
19	40	40	40	40	40	40	40	40	40	40	
20	40	40	40	40	40	40	40	40	40	16	
	768	762	800	760	720	724	724	794	692	746	7490
	Project A	Project B	Project C	Project D							
	40%	30%	20%	10%							
	2996	2247	1498	749							

Figure 6.1 Hours applied to capitalized projects

phone or email, and you don't need to ask them. You never need to interrupt their focused work time to ask them to track their hours.

What percentage of their time did each team member devote to projects A, B, C, and D? It makes no difference. They're professionals, and they will spend whatever time is necessary to get their work done. For purposes of upward reporting, you can assume that they spent approximately the correct amount of time on each project. All you need is their total work hours, and you can calculate the percentages to report for each project.

6.1.2   Aggregate numbers are approximate

You might worry that this approach will lead to inaccurate upward reporting of hours. What if the team actually spent 90% of their time on project D, but you're reporting 10%? That's theoretically possible, but in the grand scheme of things, it isn't significant. In real life, technical professionals aren't meticulous about recording their work hours in exactly the right buckets. It isn't the focus of their attention at work. It isn't what they were hired to do. They merely record hours in whichever buckets they're authorized to use, to satisfy the time-reporting system. In many cases, they're only able to enter the number of hours into each bucket that were preallocated to the projects; they couldn't report their true hours even if they wanted to. The approximate numbers you report are probably more accurate than the numbers the technical staff have been recording until now.

This is an example of how you can function as an insulating layer between teams and the organization. You're providing sufficiently accurate information to track labor costs for capitalized projects, you're providing it at the right level of detail to be useful to decision-makers, and you're doing it in a way that doesn't degrade the teams' delivery performance.

6.2   *Reporting useless but mandated metrics*

Preparing this short section has been a challenge, because it would be all too easy to say the wrong thing. Management books typically don't refer to metrics as "useless." Organizations don't typically consider anything they mandate to be useless. No one wants to be called out for requiring others to report useless numbers. No one wants to waste time reporting useless information. And yet it happens.

In addition to helping your team, you're probably required to report certain metrics outward and upward in your organization. Sometimes the required metrics aren't useful for tracking progress or for supporting process improvement. I'm not talking about metrics that the organization uses but that you don't need at the team level; those are useful, even if they aren't of direct interest to you in a team-level role. I'm talking about metrics that no one uses or *could* use. The numbers pile up on reports and presentation slides, and then they're set aside. Often, when you try to find out who uses the metrics and for what purpose, no one can tell you. Perhaps the metrics served a purpose at some time in the past. Things have changed, but the administrative requirement to report the metric remains in force. When this is the case, your *performance review* depends on reporting the required metrics, but your *actual performance* depends on measuring the things that matter and not wasting time on activities that don't add value.

As a person at the ground level with direct responsibility for delivery, how can you deal with the situation in a way that's both pragmatic and ethical? Many people face this question every day. Fortunately, there are tactical and strategic actions you can take. At the tactical level, your goal is to insulate your teams from the damaging effects of inappropriate measurement. At the strategic level, your goal is to help the organization adopt more appropriate metrics.

6.2.1 Categories of problematic metrics

You need certain measurements to help your teams deliver and improve. Your organization needs certain measurements rolled up so that management can manage programs and the organization. But sometimes the organization also requires you to roll up metrics that aren't useful to anyone. How can you ensure that you're using your time wisely? Figure 6.2 shows one way of categorizing metrics that you report outward and upward.

Metrics that are useful to *someone* have to be reported. The question is how much of your valuable time to dedicate to reporting them. Consider the lower-right quadrant in figure 6.2. This represents metrics that help you and your teams deliver. This is where you need to spend most of the time that you devote to measurement. These are the metrics you've chosen based on an analysis of the development approach, process model, and delivery mode your teams are using. You're using these metrics to steer the work and to inform process-improvement efforts.

Some of the metrics that are useful to you are also useful to others in the organization. This is represented by the upper-right quadrant in the illustration. These are a subset of the metrics you use at the team level; you don't need to report everything you

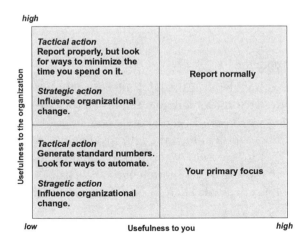

Figure 6.2 Reporting metrics outward and upward

measure for the teams. By reporting these metrics, you're making a positive contribution to the organization. But your primary focus is delivery. Therefore, you want to look for ways to automate reporting. Many organizations implement project-tracking tools that can roll up metrics automatically. Take full advantage of such tools so that you can minimize the amount of time you spend reporting this information.

The left side of figure 6.2 represents reporting requirements that aren't of direct value to your teams. The items in the upper-left quadrant are important to the organization, even if they don't directly help teams deliver. Your tactical goal is to automate the production of these numbers while insulating the teams from the administrative burden of tracking the numbers. A strategic goal, should you choose to pursue it, is to influence the decision-makers in the organization to change the measurements they're using. Techniques for organizational change are beyond the scope of this book.

The lower-left quadrant represents metrics that help no one. Why would any organization require these? It happens when people adopt a new process or methodology "by the book," without thinking about which elements of the new process are a good fit for the organization. These metrics can drive unintended behaviors. It's important that you insulate teams from dealing with this sort of reporting. At best, it will distract them from their work; at worst, it will destroy their morale.

Because the metrics in this quadrant are, by definition, not useful to anyone, it follows that the numbers can be neither right nor wrong. People report these numbers only because they're required to do so. The people who consume the numbers make note of the fact that lower-level personnel have duly reported them, and then they file the numbers away. They aren't used. When you identify metrics like this, you can automate the generation of "standard" numbers for purposes of reporting. This can't do any harm, because the numbers aren't meaningful and are never used to support business decisions. They're merely an administrative requirement.

Why haven't I listed the metrics in this dangerous category? Because different metrics are useful in different situations. A metric that's helpful in one situation may be useless in another. I can't guess which metrics will fall into this category in your context. It's up to you to understand how the work flows in your organization and measure accordingly.

6.2.2 Recognizing what's really happening

The title of this section has been the theme of the book all along, but it bears repeating. It's common for organizations to officially adopt whatever metrics are defined for the formal delivery process they've chosen. In most cases, people overlay a defined process on the organization without giving much thought to adapting the process to the organization or adapting the organization to the process. And yet most of these defined processes assume that the organization will have the characteristics that enable the process to function as intended. There's a gap between theory and reality—between intention and action.

As each metric is described in the book, there's an indication of the conditions under which the metric can be useful. This is based on three key aspects of delivery:

- *Development approach*—When scope, schedule, and budget are all fixed at the outset, the approach is *traditional*. When one or two of those factors is flexible by design, the approach is *adaptive*. Metrics that are appropriate for the approach you're using will be useful, and others won't. This is true regardless of which formal process is ostensibly in use.
- *Process model*—The process you're using is almost certainly a hybrid. The good news is that it probably resembles one of the four reference models (linear, iterative, time-boxed, or continuous flow) more closely than the other three. Metrics that apply to the closest-matching process model will be useful, and others won't.
- *Delivery mode*—Some teams are executing on discrete projects that have a beginning and an end; others are supporting a product or technical infrastructure on an ongoing basis. Metrics that apply to the delivery mode that's in use will be useful, and others won't.

Most formal processes *assume* a particular approach, process model, and delivery mode. Many organizations *assume* that when they adopt a given process, the organization automatically conforms with the expectations of that process. In those cases, some of the metrics you're required to report outward and upward may not be meaningful, and they may even be counterproductive.

6.2.3 *Beware of motivational side effects of metrics*

In addition to the mechanical aspects of delivery, it's also necessary to be aware of unintended motivational effects of metrics. Let's consider one metric in particular, because it's widely used with popular frameworks for scaling agile methods in large organizations. When using a time-boxed process model, many organizations ask teams to commit to a fixed scope of work in each iteration. This notion of *commitment* is derived from an early version of Scrum, which has since been corrected. Scrum now calls for teams to *forecast* near-term future delivery performance based on their own velocity. Unfortunately, the word *commit* continues to be used, having been adopted in other processes besides Scrum, and is included in popular agile scaling frameworks.

The problematic metric is the *percentage of the iteration commitment that the team actually delivers*. Organizations that use this metric typically set a target for performance. For example, teams might be expected to deliver 80% of the amount of work they commit to deliver in each iteration. Proponents of the metric insist that it isn't intended as a target, but in real life team members perceive it to be a target they must hit, or else.

No doubt you can see the problems with this already. Velocity is a trailing indicator intended to be used for empirical planning. The moment you set a target for it, you drive undesired behaviors. A more insidious problem is that team members will assume that their individual performance reviews depend on hitting the target.

Commitment is a serious matter, after all. We commit to our families, our communities, our professions, our countries. Commitment is life or death. Commitment is what inspires us to make personal sacrifices for our children. Commitment is what leads us to jump on a grenade to save our comrades. When required to commit, teams will sacrifice evenings, weekends, holidays, vacations, family time, and health. At least, they will do so for a while. Ultimately they will game the numbers, and the metric will be useless for its intended purpose.

6.2.4 *Understanding what the numbers mean*

Let's consider another example that's a bit less damaging. Many organizations have adopted an iterative or time-boxed process with the expectation that it will instantly enable them to deliver faster. At the same time, they don't change their expectations with regard to planning, funding, and delivery. Most of these processes were designed for adaptive development, although they can be applied to traditional development as well. The problem is measuring something that isn't happening—trying to track traditional development using metrics for adaptive development.

The metrics defined for time-boxed processes are designed to be used with adaptive development. When a project is traditional (fixed scope, schedule, and budget), then the metrics don't mean what the literature says they should mean. That doesn't necessarily make them useless, but in your position you have to be aware of what information is really tracked, or you may overlook indications of emerging delivery risks.

Time-boxed processes can be used with traditional delivery as a way to break up work into small chunks that are easy to plan, estimate, and track. In this case, velocity doesn't reflect production-ready solution increments; it merely reflects completed work items, which may be interim artifacts such as unrealized requirements specifications, unexecuted test plans, undeployed software components, or untested code units.

This isn't necessarily damaging, provided you understand what the numbers mean. You'll probably use a burn chart to forecast delivery performance based on the pseudo-velocity observations. In this context, the burn chart is showing *percentage of scope complete to date.* As you know, both types of chart look like two lines: expected performance versus actual performance to date, with a trend line showing forecast future performance. So, you can label the chart *Burn Chart* and use it as a chart of percentage complete to date. In keeping with the traditional approach, you can use the chart to try to bring the project back on plan, rather than using it to adjust scope or schedule as you would do with adaptive development.

6.3   *Summary*

To maximize their effectiveness, teams need to focus on value-add work. Part of your function is to insulate them from the distractions of administrative activities while still providing information that others in the organization need from your teams.

It's necessary to report hours worked per project for capitalized projects so the organization can enjoy the tax benefits of amortizing the cost of new software solutions. Part of your function is to provide this information without interfering with your teams' focus on delivery.

Throughout the book, I've emphasized the importance of understanding how work flows in your organization so that you can select appropriate metrics for steering and process improvement. This chapter touched on the importance of *not* using metrics that *don't* align with the approach, process model, and delivery mode in your organization. Doing so can cause undesired behavioral effects that can be both subtle and damaging.

index